INTRODUCING ISSUES WITH OPPOSING VIEWPOINTS®

Stem Cell Research

Jennifer L. Skancke, *Book Editor*

GREENHAVEN PRESS
A part of Gale, Cengage Learning

GALE
CENGAGE Learning™

Detroit • New York • San Francisco • New Haven, Conn • Waterville, Maine • London

Christine Nasso, *Publisher*
Elizabeth Des Chenes, *Managing Editor*

© 2009 Greenhaven Press, a part of Gale, Cengage Learning

For more information, contact:
Greenhaven Press
27500 Drake Rd.
Farmington Hills, MI 48331-3535
Or you can visit our Internet site at gale.cengage.com

For product information and technology assistance, contact us at

Gale Customer Support, 1-800-877-4253
For permission to use material from this text or product, submit all requests online at
www.cengage.com/permissions

Further permissions questions can be emailed to permissionrequest@cengage.com

Articles in Greenhaven Press anthologies are often edited for length to meet page
requirements. In addition, original titles of these works are changed to clearly present
the main thesis and to explicitly indicate the author's opinion. Every effort is made to
ensure that Greenhaven Press accurately reflects the original intent of the authors.
Every effort has been made to trace the owners of copyrighted material.

Cover image copyright sgame, 2008. Used under license from Shutterstock.com.

LIBRARY OF CONGRESS CATALOGING-IN-PUBLICATION DATA

Stem cell research / Jennifer L. Skancke, book editor.
    p. cm. — (Introducing issues with opposing viewpoints)
Includes bibliographical references and index.
ISBN 978-0-7377-4175-9 (hardcover)
1. Stem cells. 2. Stem cell—Research. 3. Stem cells—Social aspects. I. Skancke,
Jennifer.
QH588.S83S7382 2009
616'.02774—dc22

                                                                2008041244

Printed in the United States of America
1 2 3 4 5 6 7 12 11 10 09 08

Contents

Chapter 3: What Role Should the Government Play in Stem Cell Research?

Foreword

Indulging in a wide spectrum of ideas, beliefs, and perspectives is a critical cornerstone of democracy. After all, it is often debates over differences of opinion, such as whether to legalize abortion, how to treat prisoners, or when to enact the death penalty, that shape our society and drive it forward. Such diversity of thought is frequently regarded as the hallmark of a healthy and civilized culture. As the Reverend Clifford Schutjer of the First Congregational Church in Mansfield, Ohio, declared in a 2001 sermon, "Surrounding oneself with only like-minded people, restricting what we listen to or read only to what we find agreeable is irresponsible. Refusing to entertain doubts once we make up our minds is a subtle but deadly form of arrogance." With this advice in mind, Introducing Issues with Opposing Viewpoints books aim to open readers' minds to the critically divergent views that comprise our world's most important debates.

Introducing Issues with Opposing Viewpoints simplifies for students the enormous and often overwhelming mass of material now available via print and electronic media. Collected in every volume is an array of opinions that captures the essence of a particular controversy or topic. Introducing Issues with Opposing Viewpoints books embody the spirit of nineteenth-century journalist Charles A. Dana's axiom: "Fight for your opinions, but do not believe that they contain the whole truth, or the only truth." Absorbing such contrasting opinions teaches students to analyze the strength of an argument and compare it to its opposition. From this process readers can inform and strengthen their own opinions, or be exposed to new information that will change their minds. Introducing Issues with Opposing Viewpoints is a mosaic of different voices. The authors are statesmen, pundits, academics, journalists, corporations, and ordinary people who have felt compelled to share their experiences and ideas in a public forum. Their words have been collected from newspapers, journals, books, speeches, interviews, and the Internet, the fastest growing body of opinionated material in the world.

Introducing Issues with Opposing Viewpoints shares many of the well-known features of its critically acclaimed parent series, Opposing Viewpoints. The articles are presented in a pro/con format, allowing readers to absorb divergent perspectives side by side. Active reading questions preface each viewpoint, requiring the student to approach the material thoughtfully and carefully. Useful charts, graphs, and cartoons supplement each article. A thorough introduction provides readers with crucial background on an issue. An annotated bibliography points the reader toward articles, books, and Web sites that contain additional information on the topic. An appendix of organizations to contact contains a wide variety of charities, nonprofit organizations, political groups, and private enterprises that each hold a position on the issue at hand. Finally, a comprehensive index allows readers to locate content quickly and efficiently.

Introducing Issues with Opposing Viewpoints is also significantly different from Opposing Viewpoints. As the series title implies, its presentation will help introduce students to the concept of opposing viewpoints, and learn to use this material to aid in critical writing and debate. The series' four-color, accessible format makes the books attractive and inviting to readers of all levels. In addition, each viewpoint has been carefully edited to maximize a reader's understanding of the content. Short but thorough viewpoints capture the essence of an argument. A substantial, thought-provoking essay question placed at the end of each viewpoint asks the student to further investigate the issues raised in the viewpoint, compare and contrast two authors' arguments, or consider how one might go about forming an opinion on the topic at hand. Each viewpoint contains sidebars that include at-a-glance information and handy statistics. A Facts About section located in the back of the book further supplies students with relevant facts and figures.

Following in the tradition of the Opposing Viewpoints series, Greenhaven Press continues to provide readers with invaluable exposure to the controversial issues that shape our world. As John Stuart Mill once wrote: "The only way in which a human being can make some approach to knowing the whole of a subject is by hearing what can be said about it by persons of every variety of opinion and studying all modes in which it can be looked at by every character of mind. No wise man ever acquired his wisdom in any mode but this." It is to this principle that Introducing Issues with Opposing Viewpoints books are dedicated.

Introduction

S tem cells are "generic" cells found within the body that can make exact copies of themselves. They also have the ability to produce a number of specialized cells, such as heart muscle cells, liver tissue cells, brain tissue cells, and others. As such, stem cells are emerging as a powerful new tool for replacing destroyed or damaged tissue in various parts of the body. There are two basic types: embryonic stem cells and adult stem cells. Embryonic stem cells are obtained from aborted fetuses or embryos left over from in vitro fertilization, and adult stem cells are found in both children and adults. While adult stem cells can be turned into a limited number of other kinds of cells, embryonic stem cells have the ability to differentiate into over two hundred cell types. As a result many regard embryonic stem cells as a sort of cellular blank slate, and researchers think those cells may hold cures for conditions such as Alzheimer's and Parkinson's diseases, spinal cord injuries, heart disease, and cancer, to name just a few.

While stem cell research has garnered a lot of support from people who believe it has the potential to treat and cure disease, many others oppose the technology—especially embryonic stem cell research, because it inherently causes the destruction of an embryo. The debate that has ensued over the ethical nature of embryonic stem cell research can be summed up this way: When does human life begin, and what does it mean to be human?

The answer to this question lies in a person's opinion about when life begins and what comprises the essence of life. For some, life begins when a human displays the physical qualities that are consistent with personhood, and sometimes these are easy to identify. For example, everyone agrees that humans are people when they are infants and when they are senior citizens. Humans are such when they present the directions of their forty-six chromosomes, use their large brains and opposable thumbs, and walk erect. However, many also agree that being human is more than having arms and legs and reproductive organs. It involves having the "essence" of a human being, experiencing the thoughts, feelings, and consciousness that humans do. But are these qualities present immediately upon the fertilization of an egg by a sperm? Or does a human become a person later in development, such as when it is more developed in utero, or even later, when it is born?

People who oppose embryonic stem cell research believe that a person is a human the moment a sperm fertilizes an egg. They believe life begins when the potential for life begins—that is, it is present in the first few days after fertilization, when the rapidly dividing cells are called a blastocyst. Unless it is naturally damaged, this blastocyst has the ability to develop into an embryo, then a fetus, then an infant, then a child, then an adolescent, and then an adult. For Robert P. George, a member of the President's Council on Bioethics, the embryo should therefore be viewed as just one stage of human development. "The human embryo is not something different in kind from a human being, nor is it merely a 'potential human being,' whatever

Pictured is some of the laboratory equipment used in stem cell testing. The heart of the debate on human embryonic stem cell research centers on the crucial definition of the precise moment when life begins.

that might mean," he said. "Rather the human embryo is a human being in the embryonic stage."[1] Those who oppose embryonic stem cell research believe that all human beings deserve a right to life—no matter what stage of development.

Because embryonic stem cell research requires the dismantling of the blastocyst to reap embryonic stem cells, a process which ceases further development of an embryo, those who believe that embryos are full humans oppose the technology. For them, embryonic stem cell research is akin to wrongful killing, even murder. In fact, a 2005 Genetics and Public Policy Center survey found that 63 percent of respondents attributed a high moral status to embryos, meaning they considered embryos to have the same rights as humans, protected by the same rights that govern already born humans. Opponents argue that embryonic stem cell research violates these rights.

On the other hand, those who support embryonic stem cell research tend not to believe that a five-day-old embryo (the stage at which stem cells are harvested from it) is a full human being that should have all the rights and definitions of humanity conferred upon it. For them, embryos are a group of cells at the earliest possible stage of development. An embryo does not have a body or any body parts, nor does it have the ability to see, hear, feel, or think. It cannot live on its own and is dependent upon a host—its mother—to remain alive. From this perspective, there is more to being human than just the physical potential to grow into a human. Or, as professors Michael J. Sandel and Paul McHugh have put it, "The fact that every person began life as an embryo does not prove that embryos are persons."[2]

Furthermore, supporters of stem cell research tend to believe that to be fully human, one must possess self-consciousness, sentience (the ability to sense and respond to the world), and the ability to think. These are the qualities that define personhood for many stem cell research supporters, such as feminist scholar and theologian Rosemary Radford Ruether. As Ruether has put it: "To claim that a fertilized egg within days of conception is a human person is a totally platonic view of the human person. It means there is a human soul fully present in a tiny speck of germ plasma."[3] As such, supporters of stem cell research believe it is ethical to use embryos for research because they are not yet human. Furthermore, because embryonic stem cell research has the potential to heal or cure millions of people suffering from disease, the destruction of embryos for such a purpose is seen as not only moral, but also obligatory.

It is impossible to say whether humans will ever agree on the age or moment at which a human being comes into existence. Therefore, it is likely that stem cell research will remain an issue of intense debate for years to come. Examining whether embryos can be considered human beings is just one of the many issues explored in *Introducing Issues with Opposing Viewpoints: Stem Cell Research*. Readers will also consider arguments about whether stem cell research is moral, whether stem cell research can cure disease, and what role the government should play in funding and directing stem cell research. Readers will examine these questions in the article pairs and conclude for themselves if stem cell research should be banned or if its potential should be fully explored.

Notes

1. Robert P. George, "A Distinct Human Organism," National Public Radio, November 22, 2005. www.npr.org/templates/story/story .php?storyId=4857703.
2. Michael J. Sandel and Paul McHugh, "Embryo Ethics—the Moral Logic of Stem-Cell Research," *New England Journal of Medicine*, July 15, 2004, p. 208. http://content.nejm.org/cgi/content/full/351/ 3/207.
3. Rosemary Radford Ruether, "'Consistent Life Ethic' Is Inconsistent," *National Catholic Reporter*, November 17, 2006, p. 13.

Chapter 1

Is Stem Cell Research Moral?

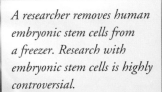

A researcher removes human embryonic stem cells from a freezer. Research with embryonic stem cells is highly controversial.

Stem Cell Research Is Immoral

William L. Saunders Jr.

In the following viewpoint William L. Saunders Jr. argues that stem cell research is immoral. Stem cell research involves using human stem cells taken from seven- to fourteen-day-old embryos. Saunders claims this practice is problematic, because an embryo is a human life—it became a human being the moment it was created. Although stem cell research can offer cures for many diseases, Saunders claims it is unethical to destroy one human for the benefit of another. Furthermore, he says that just because scientists are capable of manufacturing stem cells, society should not necessarily support and encourage what Saunders believes is unethical research. He concludes that a society that does not take a stand against destruction of human life is immoral.

William L. Saunders Jr. is a senior fellow and director of the Center for Human Life and Bioethics at the Family Research Council, a Christian nonprofit think tank

"Would any of us wish to live in a society where one class of human beings is manufactured to suit the preferences of others?"

William L. Saunders Jr., "Testimony in Support of Human Cloning Prohibition Act of 2006, Before the Health and Government Operations Committee of the Maryland House of Delegates," www.stemcell research.org, March 17, 2006.

and lobbying organization that promotes the traditional family unit based on Judeo-Christian values.

AS YOU READ, CONSIDER THE FOLLOWING QUESTIONS:

1. Why is therapeutic cloning actually nontherapeutic, according to the author?
2. According to the author, what do embryos and senior citizens have in common?
3. What does the word *manufactured* mean in the context of this viewpoint?

I welcome the opportunity to testify before you today. The issues with which this [Health and Government Operations] Committee is concerned are perhaps the most important ones facing our society.

The Family Research Council is opposed to the cloning of human beings. Our position is not based on theology or theory. Rather, it is based on straightforward scientific facts, and the necessary ethical implications that flow from those facts.

Stem Cell Research Is Lethal

Cloning is often discussed as if there were two different *kinds* of cloning, sometimes described as "therapeutic cloning" and "reproductive cloning." Both terms are, however, seriously misleading. If we do not use accurate language, it is unlikely we will be able to think clearly about the issue.

All successful cloning is reproductive. That is, once cloning results in a living single-cell human being, *reproduction*, by definition, has occurred. It does not matter for what *purpose* this cloning was accomplished —another member of the human species exists.

If a living human being has been created, then we must face this crucial question—how are we ethically obligated to treat that human being? One purpose for which cloning is pursued is to produce a subject for research experiments. Proponents call this "therapeutic cloning." This is a serious misuse of language. For even if the aim of the experiment is to produce a therapy for a disease or injury that

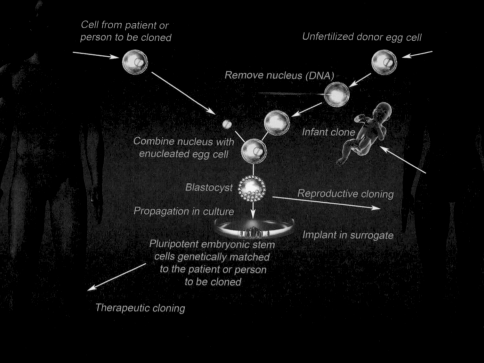

Cell from patient or person to be cloned

Unfertilized donor egg cell

Remove nucleus (DNA)

Combine nucleus with enucleated egg cell

Infant clone

Blastocyst

Reproductive cloning

Propagation in culture

Implant in surrogate

Pluripotent embryonic stem cells genetically matched to the patient or person to be cloned

Therapeutic cloning

In therapeutic cloning, DNA is inserted into an enucleated donor egg cell. This produces a blastocyst and pluripotent embryonic stem cells for culture.

was suffered by *someone else*, the research is *lethal* for the *subject* of the research (i.e., the human embryo) and is, thus, not *therapeutic* at all. It is, in its essence, *non*-therapeutic.

Such experiments have been rejected throughout Western history, and condemned by an ethical consensus expressed after World War II in the Nuremberg Code, which stated: "No experiment should be conducted where there is an a priori reason to believe that death or disabling injury will result."

However noble the ultimate purpose for which it is done, we have always agreed it is wrong to kill one human being to benefit another. Yet "therapeutic" cloning would do just that.

Embryos Are Human Beings

As counter-intuitive as it may at first appear, the reason these ethical prohibitions apply to the case of "therapeutic cloning" is because all human beings begin life as a single cell organism. Each one of us did.

Using Embryos for Science

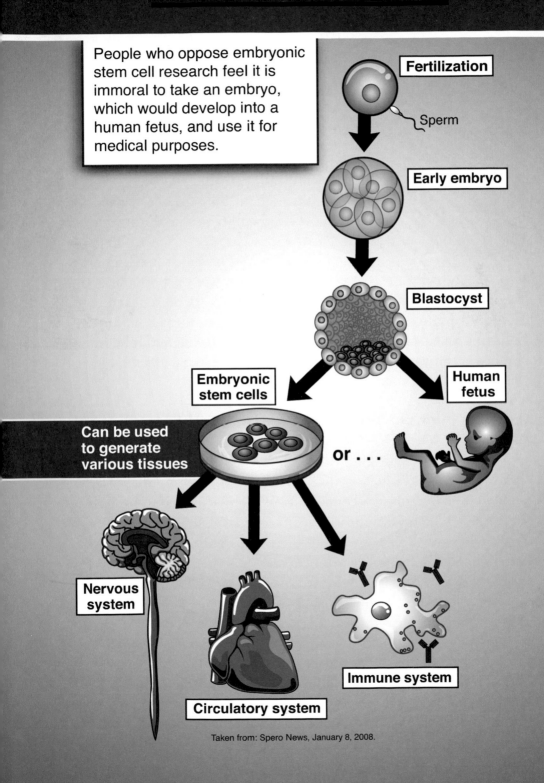

People who oppose embryonic stem cell research feel it is immoral to take an embryo, which would develop into a human fetus, and use it for medical purposes.

Fertilization

Sperm

Early embryo

Blastocyst

Embryonic stem cells

Human fetus

Can be used to generate various tissues

or . . .

Nervous system

Circulatory system

Immune system

Taken from: Spero News, January 8, 2008.

Certainly, every cell in the human body is not a human being. And left to themselves, none of those cells would become a human being.

But once a single-cell embryo or zygote has been created, whether by sexual reproduction (the exclusive means until now) or by asexual reproduction (as with cloning), that embryo is a living, distinct, genetically complete human organism which, unless interrupted, will direct its own integral growth and development through all the stages of human life —from embryo to infant to teenager to senior citizen.

Thus, as I have discussed, all cloning, for whatever purpose undertaken, is reproductive. All cloning is also unethical because it reduces a human being to an object manufactured by another. If cloning results in a live birth, excruciating problems of kinship and inheritance are posed. However, cloning for the *purpose* of lethal experiments is, in fact, the most unethical of all.

Human Cloning Will Create an Immoral Society

Whether such experiments will be permitted is an issue of great importance. The resolution of the issue will go far in determining the kind of society in which we live. Would it not destroy the hope for achieving a true human community if we permit some humans to be cloned and those cloned human beings to be destroyed in order to benefit others? Likewise, would any of us wish to live in a society where one class of human beings is manufactured to suit the preferences of others? What, indeed, will it mean to be "human" in such a society?

These are the great questions that confront you. I urge you to use this opportunity to remind the citizens of Maryland that science is, as is every other human endeavor, subject to ethical limits. Science can tell us what might be done. But it is up to citizens in a democracy to decide what will be done.

EVALUATING THE AUTHOR'S ARGUMENTS:

In this viewpoint William L. Saunders Jr. opposes stem cell research on the grounds that it is wrong to destroy life. What assumption is embedded in this argument? Do you agree with it or not, and why?

Stem Cell Research Is Moral

Robert Menendez

> *"Stem cell research has vast potential for curing diseases, alleviating suffering and saving lives."*

In the following viewpoint Robert Menendez argues that stem cell research is moral because it can cure disease and save human lives. Scientists have discovered that embryonic stem cells have the potential to cure spinal cord injuries, as well as diseases like juvenile diabetes, Alzheimer's, and Parkinson's. Menendez says that government policies that prohibit stem cell research prevent sick people from being cured. Robbing these people of a healthy, lengthy, and pain-free life is immoral and a violation of the government's responsibility to its citizens. For these reasons, Menendez concludes, it is the moral responsibility and duty of the U.S. government to allow stem cell research to go forward.

Robert Menendez has served as a Democratic senator in the U.S. Senate since 2006. He serves on the Senate committees on Banking, Housing, and Urban Affairs; Energy and Natural Resources; Budget; and Foreign Relations. He is also

Robert Menendez, "Citing Painful Connection to Alzheimer's, Senator Urges Stem Cell Research," www.menendez.senate.gov, April 10, 2007.

the chair of the Subcommittee on International Development and Foreign Assistance, Economic Affairs, and International Environmental Protection.

AS YOU READ, CONSIDER THE FOLLOWING QUESTIONS:
1. According to the author, in what way does a ban on stem cell research infringe on the rights of Americans?
2. What percentage of Americans does the author say support embryonic stem cell research?
3. Whose "moral obligation" is it to allow stem cell research, in the author's opinion?

M r. President [George W. Bush], we are back again—almost a year after Congress passed breakthrough legislation [in 2006]—discussing embryonic stem cell research and, again, I am rising in strong support of this life-saving, life-enhancing legislation.

I am a proud co-sponsor of the Stem Cell Research Enhancement Act because I believe this bill has the potential to make a profound and positive impact on the health of millions of Americans and I believe that it does so in an ethical manner.

Stem Cell Research Is Ethical

We know that embryonic stem cells have the unique ability to develop into virtually every cell and tissue in the body. And we know that numerous frozen embryos in fertility clinics remain unused by couples at the completion of their fertility treatments. Why shouldn't they be allowed to donate those embryos to federal research to save lives? We allow people to donate organs to save lives, why couldn't a couple, if they so choose, donate their frozen embryos instead of simply discarding them? We can do this ethically and still cure illnesses, enhance lives and hopefully even save lives.

But the truth is we shouldn't even be having this debate right now because if the President had done his duty last year, and not vetoed H.R. 810 [Stem Cell Research Enhancement Act], this bill would already be law—and this country's dedicated medical researchers would be well on their way to discovering treatments and cures for many of the most savage diseases afflicting us. But, when given the opportunity to carry out the will of the people, he stood for ideology and ignorance over science and research. . . .

We Owe It to Our Loved Ones

During the last Congress, President Bush vetoed H.R. 810, crushing the hopes of millions of Americans. This year [2007], I fear and suspect he will follow the same misguided path. But before he takes us down that route, one that leads to more heart breaks and suffering, I have one question—WHY?

Why is he standing in the way of research that will save lives?

Why is he keeping our parents, our children and our friends locked in wheelchairs and hospital beds?

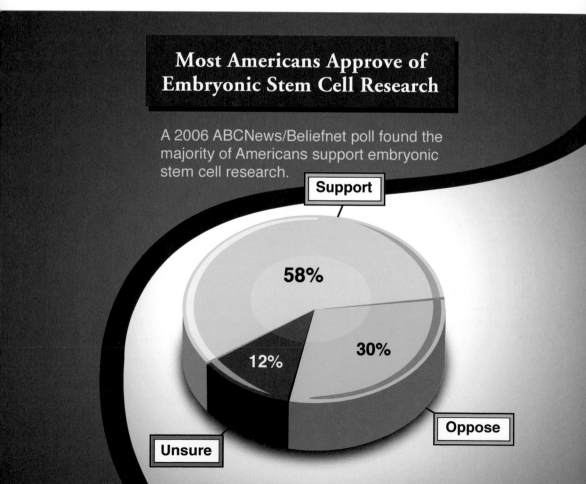

Most Americans Approve of Embryonic Stem Cell Research

A 2006 ABCNews/Beliefnet poll found the majority of Americans support embryonic stem cell research.

Support 58%

Oppose 30%

Unsure 12%

Taken from: Gary Langer, "Public Backs Stem Cell Research," ABCNews.com, June 26, 2006.

Why is he letting conservative ideology rob the lives of so many suffering Americans?

The simple fact is that, whatever the claims of those who ignore science in favor of ideology, embryonic stem cell research offers one of the most promising leaps forward in the history of medicine. Speak to those who are eager to do the research and you hear of potential cures for Juvenile Diabetes, Alzheimer's, Parkinson's disease, and spinal cord injuries. If we unlock the door to this research, we can find treatments and cures for these debilitating, painful diseases. We owe it to our parents, our children, and our grandchildren to unlock that door. . . .

Americans' Right to Stem Cell Research

The preamble of our Constitution says that all Americans have the right to 'life, liberty, and the pursuit of happiness' and I believe that this implies the freedom to be physically able. By not allowing embryonic stem cell research, we are prohibiting individuals from pursuing their rights, we are blocking them from a possible cure or treatment, and we are standing in the way of their freedom.

Last Congress, Story Landis, the interim chair of the National Institutes of Health's stem cell task force, bravely and bluntly spoke about the importance of embryonic stem cell research and the drawbacks of the current policy prohibiting research, saying:

"Science works best when scientists can pursue all avenues of research. If the cure for Parkinson's disease or Juvenile Diabetes lay behind one of four doors, wouldn't you want the option to open all four doors at once instead of one door?"

How can we tell our loved ones that their cure could be waiting behind a laboratory door but that the door is locked? We must pursue all avenues of research and unlock the potential that embryonic stem cell research holds.

But if that isn't enough—recently in a Senate HELP [Health, Education, Labor and Pensions] Committee hearing, the Director of the National Institutes of Health, Elias Zerhouni, said that the great promise of human embryonic stem cell research is being impeded by President Bush's policy. He said:

"It is in the best interest of our scientists, our science, and our country that we find ways and the nation finds a way to go full speed across adult and embryonic stem cells equally."

Stem Cell Research Offers Hope for the Suffering

So, if President Bush won't listen to his own scientists, who will he listen to?

Perhaps he will listen to the American people who are crying out in unison for a change. More than 70 percent of Americans support embryonic stem cell research. Three out of four Americans understand the hope and promise that this research provides.

This bill means that all the prayers for cures and therapies for Alzheimer's disease, muscular dystrophy, heart disease and countless

Robert Menendez, U.S. senator and author of this viewpoint, was a sponsor of the Stem Cell Research Act of 2007.

other illnesses could be answered. This bill provides a promise that families might no longer have to see a loved one suffering. This bill means hope for the individuals challenged and fighting to live a life with dignity.

I have met with children and families all over New Jersey who have shared their daily struggle with diseases and conditions that could be cured or treated if we were to pursue embryonic stem cell research.

Young children have come to my office and told me about how they have to prick themselves with a needle, administer insulin shots, or use an internal pump on the side of their body in order to keep their Juvenile Diabetes under control. These children might be freed of this grave responsibility if we support embryonic stem cell research—don't we owe them the opportunity of a better life? Don't we owe it to the husband whose wife shakes uncontrollably from Parkinson's disorder to help find a cure that will restore her body? Don't we owe it to the athletes, who told me about their life altering spinal cord injuries, to give them their freedom to walk again?

None of these individuals chose their current situation but we can choose to help get them out of it. We owe it to the American people —to the millions of Americans and their families suffering from life-altering disabilities and diseases—to demonstrate our Nation's full commitment to finding a cure and doing all we can to help their hopes and dreams come true. Stem cell research has vast potential for curing diseases, alleviating suffering and saving lives. I know my colleagues recognize the enormous potential of this research too, and it is time for the President [to] start listening. . . .

Stem Cell Research Will Save Lives

I am very passionate and dedicated to this cause because the promise of stem cell research has personally captivated my family, like it has so many other American families. My mother is suffering from Alzheimer's disease and when I look at her empty gaze and her shriveled body, I cannot help but wonder, if we had started embryonic stem cell research years ago, would she still be suffering? Would she be cured or would she at least be able to recognize her own children and grandchildren? Would she have been with me on the day I took the oath of office in this chamber?

I don't want my children to be asking the same type of questions. We cannot wait any longer.

The Stem Cell Research Enhancement Act is an ethical, life-enhancing, life-saving piece of legislation. I believe it is the moral obligation of the United States government, and the President of the United States, to allow this process—these potential cures—to be fully explored.

Embryonic stem cell research holds the promise of hope and the possible restoration of life. We owe it to current and future generations to ensure that their lives remain as bright and prosperous as today's science allows.

EVALUATING THE AUTHOR'S ARGUMENTS:

In this viewpoint Robert Menendez suggests that the government should not block Americans from reaping the benefits of stem cell research. What do you think? Should the government be allowed to prohibit science and research that can benefit human beings? Does this qualify as a violation of their rights, as the author suggests? Explain your position, quoting from the texts you have read.

Viewpoint

3

Embryos Used in Stem Cell Research Are Human Beings

William L. Saunders Jr.

"My hope is that we come to understand clearly that it is a matter of scientific fact, and not of opinion, that the embryonic organisms we are being urged to exploit and discard are, like us, human beings."

In the following viewpoint William L. Saunders Jr. argues that human beings are genetically the same at every stage of development, including the embryonic stage. The author contends that it does not matter how the embryo is produced—it is a separate individual at the moment it is created and has potential equal to that of any other living being. Saunders is senior fellow and director of the Center for Human Life and Bioethics in Washington, D.C.

AS YOU READ, CONSIDER THE FOLLOWING QUESTIONS:

1. According to the viewpoint, why was the term *pre-embryo* developed, and how was it used?
2. What is one of the arguments the author says is used to prove that embryos are not human?

William L. Saunders Jr., "Embryology: Inconvenient Facts," *First Things*, December 2004. www.firstthings .com. Reproduced by permission.

I n the ongoing debate about cloning human embryos for research, and about destroying them in order to harvest their stem cells, it is important to keep some basic facts in mind. Our moral analysis must be built upon fundamental scientific truths. If we obscure the facts, then we will not think clearly or act responsibly about these issues.

Every human being begins as a single-cell zygote, grows through the embryonic stage, then the fetal stage, is born and develops through infancy, through childhood, and through adulthood, until death. Each human being is genetically the same human being at every stage, despite changes in his or her appearance.

Fertilization Is the Starting Point

Embryologists are united on this point. Consider the following statements from standard textbooks: "Human development begins at fertilization. . . . This highly specialized, totipotent cell marked the beginning of each of us as a unique individual" (Keith L. Moore and T.V.N. Persaud); "Almost all higher animals start their lives from a single cell, the fertilized ovum (zygote). . . . The time of fertilization represents the starting point in the life history, or ontogeny, of the individual" (Bruce M. Carlson); "Although life is a continuous process, fertilization is a critical landmark because, under ordinary circumstances, a new, genetically distinct human organism is thereby formed. . . . The embryo now exists as a genetic unity" (Ronan O'Rahilly and Faiola Muller).

Normally, the embryo comes into being through sexual conception, in which the female egg cell is fertilized by a male sperm cell. In sexual reproduction the new individual gets half of its chromosomes from the nucleus of the sperm cell and half from the nucleus of the egg cell. The new organism thus produced is genetically distinct from all other human beings and has embarked upon its own distinctive development.

In addition to this normal process, we have developed laboratory techniques with which to manipulate the procreation of new human

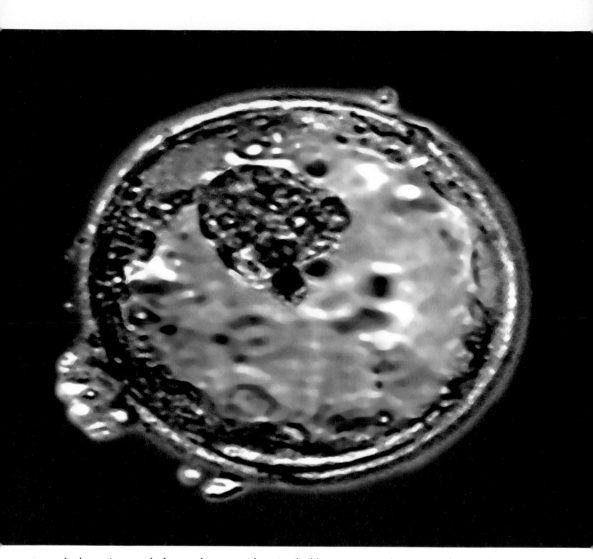

A photomicrograph shows a human embryo in the blastocyst stage. Opponents of stem cell research say that an embryo is a human being in the earliest stage of development.

organisms. One of these techniques stages the encounter of sperm with egg in a laboratory dish rather than in a woman's body. This is in vitro fertilization (IVF). Another technique is an asexual one in which no sperm is involved. Instead, an egg has its nucleus removed and replaced by a nucleus from another type of cell—a body cell. The egg is then stimulated by an electrical charge, creating a living human zygote. This is cloning, a process in which the body cell that donated the replacement nucleus supplies the chromosomes of the new human organism.

Whether the new organism is produced by [in vitro] fertilization [IVF] or by cloning, each new human organism is a distinct entity. Twins are genetic duplicates of each other, but no one would deny that each is a distinct human individual. Similarly, a clone would be a genetic duplicate of another human being, but there is no denying that it would also be a separate individual.

From its first moment, supplied with its complete set of chromosomes, each new zygote directs its own integral functioning and development. It proceeds, unless death intervenes, through every stage of human development until one day it reaches the adult stage. It will grow and it will develop and it will change its appearance, but it will never undergo a change in its basic nature. It will never grow up to be a cow or a fish. It is a human being from the first moment of its existence. As Paul Ramsey has noted, "The embryo's subsequent development may be described as a process of becoming what he already is from the moment of conception."...

Dehumanization of the Embryo

The dehumanization of the unborn was taken a step further when the concept of the "pre-embryo" was advanced. The term referred to the embryo before its implantation in the womb. Certainly the embryo at this point is "pre-implantation," and certainly implantation is a highly significant event. If the embryo does not implant, it will die; if it implants, it will receive nutrition and a suitable environment in which to live, grow, and develop. (Every human being at every stage of life similarly requires nutrition and a suitable environment.) But the critical question is: Does implantation effect a change in the nature of the thing that implants? It is clear from basic facts of embryology that it does not. In the 2001 edition of his leading textbook on embryology, Ronan O'Rahilly writes, "The term 'pre-embryo' is not used here [because] . . . it may convey the erroneous idea that a new human organism is formed only at some considerable time after fertilization. [The term] was introduced in 1986 largely for public policy reasons.". . . .

As Gilbert Meilaender has noted, the "pre-embryo" is merely the *unimplanted* embryo. In other words, it is already an embryo, and all embryos are, at first, unimplanted. An embryo subsequently implants unless something (or someone) interferes or the embryo is defective. Its life is continuous from its first moment (whether through fertilization or through cloning) until death. The term "pre-embryo" was developed and used largely, if not exclusively, to mislead: to hide scientific facts about the beginnings and unity of human life; to bolster support for a new reproductive technology; and to obtain funding for experiments on human embryos. It has led to a confused jurisprudence that treats the embryo, in certain contexts, more like property than like a human being.

Though the term "pre-embryo" has been rejected in science, the motive for its creation—to dehumanize the early embryo in order to justify its destruction—lives on. It is part of the debate over human cloning and human embryonic stem-cell research.

Embryos Will Become Humans

In the cloning debate, the attempt to deny what "everyone really knows" by finding a more accommodating language has been so convoluted that it would be amusing if lives were not at stake. First, proponents of cloning tried to deny that cloning creates a human embryo. Since, they argued, the new entity does not result from sexual reproduction, it could not be an "embryo." For reasons I have indicated (the nature of the product of cloning as a living, genetically complete, unified, self-integrating human organism in the first stage of development) few were taken in by that ploy. Even prominent advocates of embryonic stem cell research, such as John Gearhart of Johns Hopkins University, have acknowledged that the "thing" created by cloning is an embryo.

Some have asserted that the location of the thing in a Petri dish or in an IVF clinic (i.e., outside a woman's womb) means it is not an embryo. They assert that since it will never be implanted in a womb, it can never be a human being. On the Frequently Asked Questions page of the website of the Federation of American Societies for Ex-

Religious Views on Stem Cell Research

A 2005 study found that although the majority of Christians support embryonic stem cell research, they are less likely to than non-Christians due to moral and ethical objections to the use of embryos for scientific research.

Religion	Approve	Disapprove	Don't know/ no answer
Protestant	73.9	23.8	2.3
Roman Catholic	68.9	29.7	1.4
Other Christian	57.2	40.0	2.8
Fundamentalist/ Evangelical	49.6	48.0	2.4
Non-Christian	84.7	13.9	1.4
None	79.5	18.5	2.0

Taken from: Kathy L. Hudson, Joan Scott, and Ruth Faden, "Values in Conflict: Public Attitudes on Embryonic Stem Cell Research," Genetics and Public Policy Center, October 2005. www.dnapolicy.org/images/reportpdfs/2005ValuesInConflict.pdf.

perimental Biology we are told that "the cells resulting from nuclear transplantation are grown in a culture dish in the presence of special nutrients for only a few days, when they will comprise a cluster of about 120 cells that can be used to derive stem cells. Therefore, because the cells are never transferred to a uterus they cannot develop into a human being on their own."

The question-begging nature of this assertion should be evident: if the cells are "never transferred to a uterus," it is because the people in the lab choose not to transfer them. It is disingenuous for those who would deprive the embryo of the chance to be born to claim that their action changes the nature and status of the thing considered. This is like the Nazis claiming that concentration camp inmates are not human beings because the Nazis intend to destroy them during lethal experiments. The argument is a variation on the theme of "potentiality"—since the "cluster of cells" lacks the potential to be born, it is not a human being. But the fact is that every human being, including every embryo, is full of inherent potential by virtue of being human. That potential may never be realized or it may be impeded in particular cases. But that potential—to live, to grow, and to develop —is part of what it means to be a living human being. . . .

Human stem cells have indeed proven to have great value in the invention of new medical treatments, though it is significant that the only treatments developed to date have involved stem cells acquired nondestructively from nonembryonic sources, including adult donors. Therapies involving the use of adult stem cells are already numerous, whereas therapies derived from embryonic stem cells are still only theoretical. . . . Wesley J. Smith has called the media coverage of advances in adult-stem-cell regenerative therapies "grudging," and notes that the favored theme in much media coverage is that embryos hold the key to the future.

Nonetheless, the public is becoming aware that stem cells can be obtained, nondestructively, from adults. And we are also becoming aware that the harvesting of stem cells from embryos cannot be accomplished without causing those embryos to cease to exist as organisms—that is, without killing them. My hope is that we come to understand clearly that it is a matter of scientific fact, and not of opinion, that the embryonic organisms we are being urged to exploit and discard are, like us, human beings.

> **EVALUATING THE AUTHOR'S ARGUMENTS:**
>
> This article was originally published in the religious journal *First Things*. Do you believe the source has an effect on the validity of the author's arguments? Why or why not? Explain your reasoning.

Viewpoint

4

Embryos Used in Stem Cell Research Are Not Human Beings

Michael J. Sandel and Paul McHugh

"The fact that every person began life as an embryo does not prove that embryos are persons."

In the following viewpoint Michael J. Sandel and Paul McHugh argue that while embryos used in stem cell research have the potential to be human beings, they are not full-fledged persons. While humans develop from embryos, embryos themselves are different. An embryo is a simple group of cells in the earliest stage of human development. This is very different from being a human, or even a baby, because embryos are incapable of experiencing life the way humans at the infant, child, or adult stages do. For example, embryos do not yet have a consciousness, are incapable of feeling emotions or physical sensations, and do not possess other qualities that make humans human. These qualities develop over time, as an embryo matures into an infant. For all of these reasons, Sandel and

Michael J. Sandel and Paul McHugh, "Embryo Ethics—the Moral Logic of Stem-Cell Research," *New England Journal of Medicine*, July 15, 2004.

McHugh argue that critics who equate embryos with humans hinder the biomedical promise of stem cell research and threaten countless human lives in the process.

Michael J. Sandel is a professor of government at Harvard University. Paul McHugh is a professor of psychiatry at Johns Hopkins University School of Medicine. Both serve on the President's Council on Bioethics.

AS YOU READ, CONSIDER THE FOLLOWING QUESTIONS:

1. In what way are embryos and humans like acorns and oak trees, according to the authors?
2. According to the authors, if it is immoral to conduct stem cell research on embryos, then it should also be immoral to use embryos for what medical procedure?
3. What are three ways in which the authors suggest the government could protect stem cell research from immorality?

A t first glance, the case for federal funding of embryonic stem-cell research seems too obvious to need defending. Why should the government refuse to support research that holds promise for the treatment and cure of devastating conditions such as Parkinson's disease, Alzheimer's disease, diabetes, and spinal cord injury? Critics of stem-cell research offer two main objections: some hold that despite its worthy ends, stem-cell research is wrong because it involves the destruction of human embryos; others worry that even if research on embryos is not wrong in itself, it will open the way to a slippery slope of dehumanizing practices, such as embryo farms, cloned babies, the use of fetuses for spare parts, and the commodification of human life.

Embryos and Humans Are "Different Kinds of Things"

Neither objection is ultimately persuasive, though each raises questions that proponents of stem-cell research should take seriously. Consider the first objection. Those who make it begin by arguing, rightly, that biomedical ethics is not only about ends but also about means; even research that achieves great good is unjustified if it comes at the price of violating fundamental human rights. For example, the ghoulish experiments of Nazi doctors would not be morally justified even if they resulted in discoveries that alleviated human suffering.

Few would dispute the idea that respect for human dignity imposes certain moral constraints on medical research. The question is whether the destruction of human embryos in stem-cell research amounts to the killing of human beings. The "embryo objection" insists that it does. For those who adhere to this view, extracting stem cells from a blastocyst is morally equivalent to yanking organs from a baby to save other people's lives.

Some base this conclusion on the religious belief that ensoulment occurs at conception. Others try to defend it without recourse to religion, by the following line of reasoning: Each of us began life as an embryo. If our lives are worthy of respect, and hence inviolable, simply by virtue of our humanity, one would be mistaken to think that at some younger age or earlier stage of development we were not worthy of respect. Unless we can point to a definitive moment in the passage from conception to birth that marks the emergence of the human person, this argument claims, we must regard embryos as possessing the same inviolability as fully developed human beings.

But this argument is flawed. The fact that every person began life as an embryo does not prove that embryos are persons. Consider an analogy: although every oak tree was once an acorn, it does not follow that acorns are oak trees, or that I should treat the loss of an acorn eaten by a squirrel in my front yard as the same kind of loss as the death of an oak tree felled by a storm. Despite their developmental continuity, acorns and oak trees are different kinds of things. So are human embryos and human beings. Sentient creatures make claims on us that nonsentient ones do not; beings capable of experience and consciousness make higher claims still. Human life develops by degrees.

Embryonic Stem Cell Research Is Not Murder

Those who view embryos as persons often assume that the only alternative is to treat them with moral indifference. But one need not regard the embryo as a full human being in order to accord it a certain respect. To regard an embryo as a mere thing, open to any use we desire or devise, does, it seems to me, miss its significance as potential human life. Few would favor the wanton destruction of embryos or the use of embryos for the purpose of developing a new line of cosmetics. Personhood is not the only warrant for respect. For example, we consider it an act of disrespect when a hiker carves his initials in an ancient sequoia—not because we regard the sequoia as a person, but because we regard it as a natural wonder worthy of appreciation and awe. To respect the old-growth forest does not mean that no tree may ever be felled or harvested for human purposes. Respecting the forest may be consistent with using it. But the purposes should be weighty and appropriate to the wondrous nature of the thing.

Proponents of stem cell research say that a human embryo in a petri dish does not have the same moral status as a person.

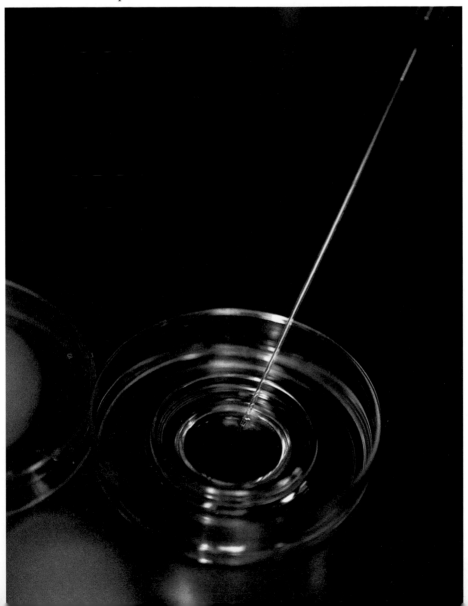

The notion that an embryo in a petri dish has the same moral status as a person can be challenged on further grounds. Perhaps the best way to see its implausibility is to play out its full implications. First, if harvesting stem cells from a blastocyst were truly on a par with harvesting organs from a baby, then the morally responsible policy would be to ban it, not merely deny it federal funding. If some doctors made a practice of killing children to get organs for transplantation, no one would take the position that the infanticide should be ineligible for federal funding but allowed to continue in the private sector. If we were persuaded that embryonic stem-cell research were tantamount to infanticide, we would not only ban it but treat it as a grisly form of murder and subject scientists who performed it to criminal punishment.

Embryos Cannot Be Equated with Infants

Second, viewing the embryo as a person rules out not only stem-cell research, but all fertility treatments that involve the creation and discarding of excess embryos. In order to increase pregnancy rates and spare women the ordeal of repeated attempts, most in vitro fertilization clinics create more fertilized eggs than are ultimately implanted. Excess embryos are typically frozen indefinitely or discarded. (A small number are donated for stem-cell research.) But if it is immoral to sacrifice embryos for the sake of curing or treating devastating diseases, it is also immoral to sacrifice them for the sake of treating infertility.

Third, defenders of in vitro fertilization point out that embryo loss in assisted reproduction is less frequent than in natural pregnancy, in which more than half of all fertilized eggs either fail to implant or are otherwise lost. This fact highlights a further difficulty with the view that equates embryos and persons. If natural procreation entails the loss of some embryos for every successful birth, perhaps we should worry less about the loss of embryos that occurs in in vitro fertilization and stem-cell research. Those who view embryos

BUSH, BATHWATER & BABIES

IRRATIONAL MORALITY

BENEFITS OF EMBRYONIC STEM CELL RESEARCH

© 2007 MONTE WOLVERTON

caglecartoons.com

© 2007 Monte Wolverton and PoliticalCartoons.com.

as persons might reply that high infant mortality would not justify infanticide. But the way we respond to the natural loss of embryos suggests that we do not regard this event as the moral or religious equivalent of the death of infants. Even those religious traditions that are the most solicitous of nascent human life do not mandate the same burial rituals and mourning rites for the loss of an embryo as for the death of a child. Moreover, if the embryo loss that accompanies natural procreation were the moral equivalent of infant death, then pregnancy would have to be regarded as a public health crisis of epidemic proportions; alleviating natural embryo loss would be a more urgent moral cause than abortion, in vitro fertilization, and stem-cell research combined.

If Embryos Were Humans, Stem Cell Research Would Be Banned

Even critics of stem-cell research hesitate to embrace the full implications of the embryo objection. President George W. Bush has prohibited federal funding for research on embryonic stem-cell lines derived after August 9, 2001, but has not sought to ban such research, nor has he called on scientists to desist from it. And as the stem-cell debate heats up in Congress, even outspoken opponents of embryo research have not mounted a national campaign to ban in vitro fertilization or to prohibit fertility clinics from creating and discarding excess embryos. This does not mean that their positions are unprincipled—only that their positions cannot rest on the principle that embryos are inviolable.

Regulation Can Protect Stem Cell Research

What else could justify restricting federal funding for stem-cell research? It might be the worry, mentioned above, that embryo research will lead down a slippery slope of exploitation and abuse. This objection raises legitimate concerns, but curtailing stem-cell research is the wrong way to address them. Congress can stave off the slippery slope by enacting sensible regulations, beginning with a simple ban on human reproductive cloning. Following the approach adopted by the United Kingdom, Congress might also require that research embryos not be allowed to develop beyond 14 days, restrict the commodification of embryos and gametes [sperm and egg], and establish a stem-cell bank to prevent proprietary interests from monopolizing access to stem-cell lines. Regulations such as these could save us from slouching toward a brave new world as we seek to redeem the great biomedical promise of our time.

EVALUATING THE AUTHORS' ARGUMENTS:

The author of the previous viewpoint argued that human embryos are persons that deserve the same respect as that of an infant, adolescent, or adult human being. After reading this viewpoint, how do you think Michael J. Sandel and Paul McHugh might respond to that claim? Support your answer with evidence from both texts.

Stem Cell Research Is Murder

Judie Brown

"Even if it were successful and even if killing human embryonic children produced miraculous cures, it is always immoral to pursue the research."

In the following viewpoint Judie Brown argues that using human embryos in stem cell research is murder. Brown claims that destroying an embryo for stem cell research is the equivalent to harvesting organs from a one-year-old child. The only difference between an embryonic child and an infant, she says, is size and age. The argument that embryos are merely a clump of cells that do not have spinal nerves or the ability to be self-aware holds no merit, she argues, and questions whether any living person would have chosen to give up their life at the embryonic stage for the sake of science. For these reasons, she argues that destroying embryos that do not have a choice in the matter is murder. As such, Brown concludes that embryos should not be used for stem cell research.

Judie Brown is president and cofounder of American Life League, the nation's largest grassroots pro-life educational organization. She is also currently serving her

Judie Brown, "We Deserve Better than Embryonic Stem Cell Research Fraud," *Renew America*, January 10, 2007. www.renewamerica.us. Reproduced by permission.

second five-year term as a member of the Pontifical Academy for Life in Rome.

AS YOU READ, CONSIDER THE FOLLOWING QUESTIONS:

1. How does the author interpret the comments of Congressman Michael Castle?
2. What three methods does Brown say offer more promise for curing disease than stem cells?
3. What breakthroughs in Toronto, Illinois, and Great Britain does the author discuss, and how do they factor into her argument?

Very early in my life I learned a valuable lesson: when you manipulate the truth, you not only distort the subject you are discussing but you bring shame upon yourself as well.

As I have read the various news reports dealing with the [Democratic majority leader Nancy] Pelosi push for limitless funding of human embryonic stem cell research, I have been reminded of that lesson more times than I care to tabulate. And it consistently amazes me that those who lead the cheer for human embryonic stem cell research appear oblivious to the source of real progress and downright comatose about the abysmal results of the very research they favor.

A Human Embryo Is the Same as a Human Being

But perhaps the fundamental problem is far more serious. You see not once in all the discussion over the congressional bill, H.R. 3, "Stem Cell Research Enhancement Act of 2007," have we experienced an actual biology lesson on the identity of the human embryo. We have been told that these embryos are "leftovers" and that they are going to be "discarded anyway."

For example, we have heard Congressman Michael Castle (R-DE) say that the race to cure "tens of millions of patients suffering worldwide from diseases such as Juvenile Diabetes, Parkinson's, Alzheimer's, cancer and AIDS" makes increased funding for human embryonic stem cell research a must! His January 9 [2007] statement went on to justify the killing of human embryos by telling the public that "the decision to discard the embryo which will be used for the research will already have been made and only then can the couple donate an embryo for research."

Let's state that in a different way so that we get the full meaning of this deceptively phrased statement. What if Castle had said "The decision to throw away the one-year-old baby which will be used for the research will already have been made and only then can the parents donate their child's body for research?"

Think about it. Would the public sit still for that kind of research? Of course not. But what is the actual difference between a one-year-old child and an embryonic child? Size and age. That is the only difference. The human being who is described as an embryo is no different than the human being who is described as a one year old child.

As MIT [Massachusetts Institute of Technology] stem cell scientist Dr. James Sherley said, "Whether or not the embryo has yet developed spinal nerves or self-awareness is an irrelevant point made to distract and confuse. I challenge the promoters of human embryonic stem cell research to justify why another human embryonic life is less worthy than their own was."

Supporters of Embryonic Stem Cell Research Are Misinformed

The language of the human embryonic stem cell research crowd has been specifically designed to deny the truth, to dismiss the human embryo as nothing more than a clump of cells and to make those of us who favor protecting such individuals from death and destruction appear to be unfeeling, heartless simpletons who do not care about curing diseases or relieving suffering people of their pain and agony.

But these same individuals will not take a moment out to study the facts about stem cell research, the advances that have been made using adult stem cells, cord blood stem cells or, most recently, stem cells taken from amniotic fluid. In fact, the rush to deny such successes is so transparent; even the lead scientist for the amniotic fluid stem cell breakthrough took time out of his busy schedule to let the world know that he wants Congress to fund embryonic stem cell research and that the legislation in question needs to pass! Why? Because, in my humble view, he has joined the ranks of those who believe that

Significant Events in Stem Cell Research

1978	The United States establishes an Ethics Advisory Board (EAB) whose review is required for federal funding of in vitro fertilization research.
1981	First American in vitro fertilization (IVF) baby, Elizabeth Carr, is born in Norfolk, VA.
1994	The National Institutes of Health (NIH) establishes the Human Embryo Research Panel, which recommends federal funding for embryo research using either "spare" embryos from IVF with parental consent, or embryos created solely for research purposes.
1994	President Bill Clinton says he does "not believe that federal funds should be used to support the creation of human embryos for research purposes" and directs the National Institutes of Health (NIH) not to support such research.
1995	Researchers at the University of Wisconsin isolate the first embryonic stem cells in rhesus macaque monkeys. The research shows it is possible to derive embryonic stem cells from primates, including humans.
1996	Congress passes the Dickey-Wicker Amendment banning NIH funding of human embryo research.
1997	The first successful cloning of a mammal, Dolly the sheep, is achieved by scientists in Edinburgh, Scotland.
1998	Researchers at the University of Wisconsin–Madison are the first to report the isolation of human embryonic stem cells.
1999	The Department of Health and Human Services concludes that public funds can be used for research on human embryonic stem cells derived using only private funds.
2000	The NIH releases guidelines allowing federally funded research on human embryonic stem cells derived in the private sector.
2001	President Bush allows federal funding of human embryonic stem cell research to proceed but only on cell lines already in existence worldwide, which were derived from leftover embryos from fertility clinics.
2001	President Bush also establishes the President's Council on Bioethics to study ethical issues in biomedical sciences and to oversee all federally funded human embryonic stem cell research.
2004	Korean scientists clone thirty human embryos and harvest stem cells from them. One new stem cell line is created.

2004	Californians pass Proposition 71, allowing the state to spend $3 billion over ten years to fund human embryonic stem cell research.
2005	Researchers at Seoul National University in South Korea create eleven human embryonic stem cell lines from cloned human embryos. The lines are used to study human disease and therapies but are off-limits to federally funded American scientists as per U.S. policy restricting stem cell research to lines that were created prior to 2001.
2005	Researchers at Kingston University in England discover a new category of stem cell derived from umbilical cord blood.
2005	The state of New Jersey announces it will fund a $150 million stem cell research center.
2005	The President's Council on Bioethics publishes "Alternative Sources of Pluripotent Stem Cells" describing theoretical methods for obtaining embryonic stem cells without destroying embryos.
2005	Connecticut lawmakers earmark $100 million for stem cell research over ten years to compete with biotech industries in California and New Jersey.
2005	Illinois governor Rod Blagojevich uses an executive order to circumvent the state legislature to dedicate $10 million for stem cell research.
2005	Senate majority leader Bill Frist (R-TN) breaks with President Bush and announces his support to loosen federal restrictions on human embryonic stem cell research.
2006	Scientists in England create the first ever artificial liver cells using umbilical cord blood stem cells.
2007	Scientists at Wake Forest University report discovery of a new type of stem cell in amniotic fluid. This may potentially provide an alternative to embryonic stem cells for use in research and therapy.
2007	Research reported by three different groups shows that adult skin cells can be reprogrammed to an embryonic state in mice.

Taken from: Compiled by the editor from a variety of sources.

it is all about the money . . . the more dollars the better, regardless of whether the particular research being funded is actually producing promised results.

One commentator even correctly suggested that scientific claims are inflated specifically to garner more and more money.

Non-Embryonic Stem Cells Are Effective in Treating Disease

Yet anyone who would take the time to review the record would immediately notice that the best and most promising research being done today uses either the patient's own stem cells, cord blood stem cells or no stem cells of any kind. There is nothing to indicate that human embryonic stem cell research is effectively producing any promising results.

State after state is authorizing huge expenditures of taxpayer dollars so that they can remain in the race. Huge biotech companies are investing millions in the research, and now Congress wants to

A technician removes cells from a human embryo to generate stem cells. Critics contend that this is a form of murder.

expand that funding base to include millions of federal tax dollars as well. For what? I ask you.

In Toronto Canada researchers have discovered a cure for diabetes in mice. Not a single stem cell of any kind was used in the initial research, yet few have heard about the work of Fr. Hans Michael Dosch and Dr. Michael Dalter whose injection of the active ingredient in hot chili peppers into the pancreatic sensory nerves of mice produced the amazing discovery. Yet not a single human embryo was killed.

In Illinois a three-year-old child suffering from leukemia was given a lifesaving infusion of her own cord blood which saved her life and now at age six she is thriving. Not a single human embryo was killed.

In Great Britain researchers have discovered that mesenchymal stem cells from adult bone marrow can effectively regenerate spinal discs. Not a single human embryo was killed.

Embryonic Children Should Not Be Sacrificed in the Name of False Science

Human embryonic stem cell research is all hype and little hope. But you know, even if it were successful and even if killing human embryonic children produced miraculous cures, it is always immoral to pursue the research.

And one final note for those who get their news from the major media. The [George W.] Bush Administration has never banned human embryonic stem cell research; it has permitted federal funding for such research as long as the stem cell lines were in existence prior to the pronouncement President Bush made in August of 2001. The Bush Administration has never opposed private sector funding of such research and has never condemned it in any way.

The bottom line in all this is that hype has far exceeded facts. The bogey man created by human embryonic stem cell fanatics is the individual lawmaker or activist who chooses to rely on truth and not to sacrifice one single embryonic child in the process of fulfilling false dreams or advancing fabricated claims of hope for the ill and the dying.

The agenda of the proponents of such research may never be fully understood. But there is one thing that has become crystal clear in all the mainstream media coverage: Not a single shred of factual evidence is being sought or reported.

If killing millions of innocent human persons isn't scandal enough, then American taxpayers should be outraged by human embryonic stem [cell] research because it is science fiction. We deserve better.

EVALUATING THE AUTHOR'S ARGUMENTS:

Judie Brown argues in this viewpoint that research scientists commit murder when they use embryonic stem cells. To make her argument, the author quotes from several sources. Who has the author quoted, and how has she used these quotations to build her argument?

Stem Cell Research Is Not Murder

David Holcberg and Alex Epstein

"Embryos used in embryonic stem cell research are manifestly not human beings— not in any rational sense of the term."

In the following viewpoint David Holcberg and Alex Epstein argue that stem cell research is not murder. Opponents of stem cell research claim that embryos are human beings with a right to life. However, Holcberg and Epstein explain that rights are given to humans so they can think, act, work, feel, love, and live in freedom. Since embryos are merely clusters of a few hundred undifferentiated cells that do not see, hear, feel, or think, the authors claim the concept of rights does not apply to them. As such, the authors argue that embryos do not have rights that can be infringed upon. In this way, using embryonic cells for research cannot equal murder. In fact, the authors conclude that the real violation of rights comes from denying scientists the opportunity to pursue lifesaving cures for humans suffering from illness and disease.

David Holcberg is a media research and op-ed specialist, and Alex Epstein is a junior fellow at the Ayn Rand Institute in

David Holcberg and Alex Epstein, "The Anti-Life Opposition to Embryonic Stem Cell Research," Ayn Rand Institute, May 31, 2005. Reproduced by permission.

Irvine, California. The institute promotes objectivism, the philosophy of Ayn Rand, who is the author of *Atlas Shrugged* and *The Fountainhead*.

AS YOU READ, CONSIDER THE FOLLOWING QUESTIONS:
1. What is the difference, in the authors' opinion, between a *potential* and an *actual* human being?
2. What is the purpose of rights, according to Holcberg and Epstein?
3. Why do the authors think "pro-lifers" is an ironic term to apply to those who oppose stem cell research?

It is widely known that embryonic stem cell research has the potential to revolutionize medicine and save millions of lives. Yet many Congressmen are frantically working to defeat a measure that would expand federal financing of this research. Why are they (and so many others) opposing embryonic stem cell research—and doing so under the banner of being "pro-life"?

Embryos Are Not Human Beings

The opponents of embryonic stem cell research claim that their position is rooted in "respect for human life." They say that the embryos destroyed in the process of extracting stem cells are human beings with a right to life.

But embryos used in embryonic stem cell research are manifestly not human beings—not in any rational sense of the term. These embryos are smaller than a grain of sand, and consist of at most a few hundred undifferentiated cells. They have no body or body parts. They do not see, hear, feel, or think. While they have the *potential* to become human beings—if implanted in a woman's uterus and brought to term—they are nowhere near *actual* human beings.

It Is Not Rational to Attribute Rights to Embryos

What, then, is the "pro-lifers'" reason for regarding these collections of cells as sacred and attributing rights to them? Religious dogma.

The "pro-lifers" accept on faith the belief that rights are a divine creation: a gift from an unknowable supernatural being bestowed on embryos at conception (which many extend to embryos "conceived" in a beaker). The most prominent example of this view is the official doctrine of the Catholic Church, which declares to its followers that an embryo "is to be respected and treated as a person from the moment of conception; and therefore from that same moment his rights as a person must be recognized."

But rights are not some supernatural construct, mystically granted by the will of "God." They are this-worldly principles of proper political interaction rooted in man's rational nature. Rights recognize the fact that men can only live successfully and happily among one another if they are free from the initiation of force against them. Rights exist to protect and further human life. Rights enable individual men to think, act, produce and trade, live and love in freedom. The principle of rights is utterly inapplicable to tiny, pre-human clusters of cells that are incapable of such actions.

The authors of this viewpoint contend that stem cells (shown) that are extracted from embryos are not yet human beings.

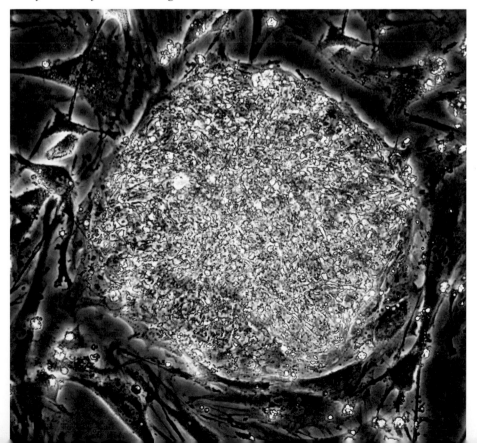

© 2006 Monte Wolverton and PoliticalCartoons.com.

Restricting Stem Cell Research Violates Scientists' Rights

In fact, to attribute rights to embryos is to call for the violation of actual rights. Since the purpose of rights is to enable individuals to secure their well-being, a crucial right, inherent in the right to liberty and property, is the right to do scientific research in pursuit of new medical treatments. To deprive scientists of the freedom to use clusters of cells to do such research is to violate their rights—as well as the rights of all who would contribute to, invest in, or benefit from this research.

And to the extent that rights are violated in this way, we can expect deadly results. The political pressure against embryonic stem cell research is already discouraging many scientists and businessmen from investing their time and resources in its pursuit. If this research can lead, as scientists believe, to the ability to create new tissues and organs to replace damaged ones, any obstacles placed in its path will unnecessarily delay the discovery of new cures and treatments for diseases such as Parkinson's, Alzheimer's, osteoporosis, and diabetes. Every day that this potentially life-saving research is delayed is another day that will go by before new treatments become available to ease the suffering and save the lives of countless individuals. And if the "pro-lifers" ever achieve the ban they seek on embryonic stem cell research, millions upon millions of human beings, living or yet to be born, might be deprived of healthier, happier, and longer lives.

The enemies of embryonic stem cell research know this, but are unmoved. They are brazenly willing to force countless human beings to suffer and die for lack of treatments, so that clusters of cells remain untouched.

Embryonic Stem Cell Research Is Necessary to Save Lives

To call such a stance "pro-life" is beyond absurd. Their allegiance is not to human life or to human rights, but to their anti-life dogma. If these enemies of human life wish to deprive themselves of the benefits of stem cell research, they should be free to do so and die faithful to the last. But any attempt to impose their religious dogma on the rest of the population is both evil and unconstitutional. In the name of the actual sanctity of human life and the inviolability of rights, embryonic stem cell research must be allowed to proceed unimpeded. Our lives may depend on it.

EVALUATING THE AUTHORS' ARGUMENTS:

David Holcberg and Alex Epstein argue that depriving humans the opportunity to benefit from stem cell research is more deadly than using nonhuman embryos for research. Clarify what they mean by this. Do you think they are right? Explain your answer thoroughly. Then, list how you think each of the other authors in this chapter would respond to this suggestion.

Chapter 2

Can Stem Cell Research Cure Disease?

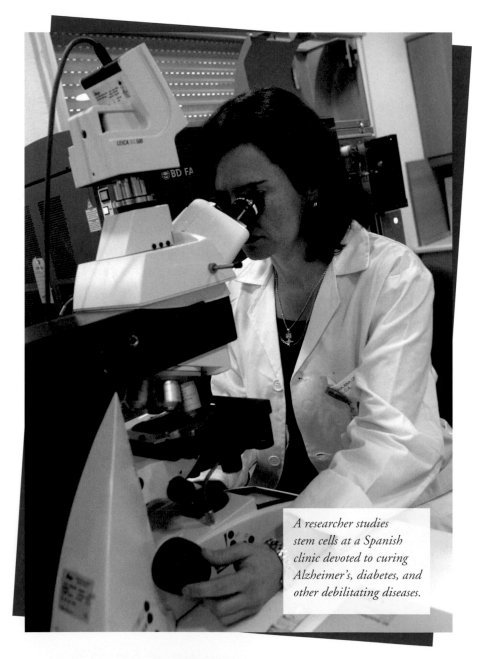

A researcher studies stem cells at a Spanish clinic devoted to curing Alzheimer's, diabetes, and other debilitating diseases.

Stem Cell Research Can Cure Many Diseases

Barack Obama

"Stem cells have the potential to treat blood disorders, lung diseases, and heart damage."

In the following viewpoint Barack Obama argues that stem cell research can cure many diseases that afflict millions of Americans each year. He explains that debilitating conditions such as Alzheimer's disease, diabetes, blood diseases, heart problems, and spinal cord injuries cause the death and suffering of millions of Americans and their families. Some of these people live in pain, and others experience a lesser quality of life as a result of their disease. But it has been discovered that stem cells have the potential to treat these diseases, offering hope, health, and happiness to millions. As such, Obama believes it is critical that stem cell research be expanded so that those suffering from disease might one day have an opportunity to live a pain-free and healthy life. The best way to do this is to use embryos from fertility clinics that would have otherwise been discarded, the

Barack Obama, "Statement of Support for Stem Cell Research," http://obama.senate.gov, July 17, 2006.

author suggests. This way, embryos that would have been thrown out can help save lives and cure disease.

Barack Obama is the forty-fourth president of the United States. He previously served as a Democratic senator from Illinois and on the Illinois state Senate.

AS YOU READ, CONSIDER THE FOLLOWING QUESTIONS:

1. How many Americans does the author report are diagnosed with diabetes each year?
2. How many embryos are stored in how many medical facilities throughout the United States, according to Obama?
3. What disease does Obama say the government helped cure fifty years ago after stepping in with support and funding?

M r. President, [George W. Bush], a few weeks ago [June 2006] I was visited by two of my constituents—Mary Schneider and her son Ryan.

When Ryan was just two years old, his parents and doctors noted severe delays in his motor and speech development, and he was diagnosed with cerebral palsy. His parents were devastated, as the prognosis for many children with cerebral palsy is quite grim, and given the severity of Ryan's condition, his doctors didn't have much hope for his improvement.

Yet, his parents had hope. Because when Ryan was born, his parents had saved his cord blood, a viable but limited source of stem cells. They found a doctor at Duke University who was willing to perform an experimental infusion with these cells to see if they might improve his condition.

They did. In fact, they seem to have cured him.

Within months of the infusion, Ryan was able to speak, use his arms, and eat normally, just like any other child—miracles his family had once only dreamed of.

Ryan's story exemplifies the power and the promise of stem cells to treat and cure the millions of Americans who are suffering from catastrophic, debilitating and life-threatening diseases and health conditions.

Stem Cell Research Can Save Lives

Each year, 100,000 Americans will develop Alzheimer's disease. Over 1 million adults will be diagnosed with diabetes this year, which can lead to complications such as blindness, damaged nerves and loss of kidney function. And there are far too many individuals with spinal cord injuries who are struggling to maintain mobility and independence.

For most of our history, medicine has offered little hope of recovery to individuals affected by these and other devastating illnesses and injuries.

Until now.

Recent developments in stem cell research may hold the key to improved treatments, if not cures, for those affected by Alzheimer's disease, diabetes, spinal cord injury and countless other conditions.

Many men, women and children who are cancer survivors are already familiar with the life-saving applications of adult stem cell research. Patients with leukemia or lymphoma often undergo bone marrow transplants, a type of stem cell transplant, which can significantly prolong life, or permanently get rid of the cancer. This therapy has been used successfully for decades, and is saving lives every day.

Adult Stem Cells Have Limitations

Yet this breakthrough has its serious limitations. Adult stem cells, such as those used in bone marrow transplants, can only be collected in small quantities, may not be a match for the patient, and have limited ability to transform into specialized cells.

Cord blood, like the kind Ryan used, has limitations as well. If, for example, young Ryan's condition should deteriorate or he should develop another illness, there simply are not enough cord blood cells left for a second use. His mother has told us that the few remaining cells

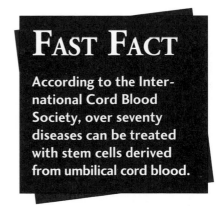

FAST FACT

According to the International Cord Blood Society, over seventy diseases can be treated with stem cells derived from umbilical cord blood.

would have to be cloned to get enough cells for future use, or they would have to obtain stem cells from another source.

These and other difficulties are the reasons why scientists have started to explore other types and other sources for stem cells, including embryonic stem cell research.

Embryonic Stem Cells Have Potential to Treat Disease

Embryonic stem cells can be obtained from a number of sources, including in vitro fertilization. At this very moment, there are over 400,000 embryos being stored in over 400 facilities throughout the United States. The majority of these are reserved for infertile couples. However, many of these embryos will go unused, destined for per-

As the forty-fourth president, Barack Obama is expected to make significant changes to the United States' stem cell research policy.

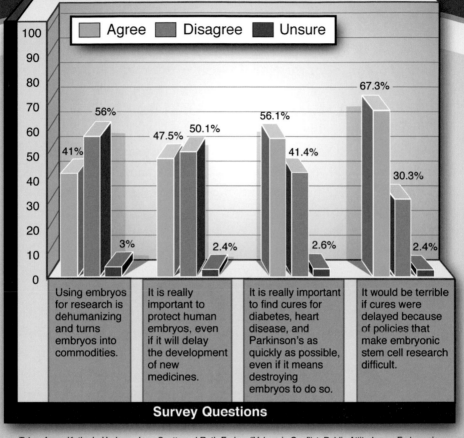

Americans Want to Cure Disease with Embryonic Stem Cell Research

The majority of Americans approve of using embryos for research if it means funding cures and treatments for conditions such as diabetes, Parkinson's, and heart disease.

Legend: Agree · Disagree · Unsure

Survey Questions	Agree	Disagree	Unsure
Using embryos for research is dehumanizing and turns embryos into commodities.	41%	56%	3%
It is really important to protect human embryos, even if it will delay the development of new medicines.	47.5%	50.1%	2.4%
It is really important to find cures for diabetes, heart disease, and Parkinson's as quickly as possible, even if it means destroying embryos to do so.	56.1%	41.4%	2.6%
It would be terrible if cures were delayed because of policies that make embryonic stem cell research difficult.	67.3%	30.3%	2.4%

Taken from: Kathy L. Hudson, Joan Scott, and Ruth Faden, "Values in Conflict: Public Attitudes on Embryonic Stem Cell Research," Genetics and Public Policy Center, October 2005. www.dnapolicy.org/images/reportpdfs/2005ValuesInConflict.pdf.

manent storage in a freezer or disposal. We should expand and accelerate research using these embryos, just as we should continue to explore the viability of adult stem cell use and cord blood use.

All over the country, exciting progress is being made in the area of embryonic stem cell research. At the University of Illinois, they're finding that stem cells have the potential to treat blood disorders, lung diseases, and heart damage.

At Johns Hopkins, researchers were able to use mouse embryonic stem cells to repair damaged nerves and restore mobility in paralyzed rats. One can't help but think that it's a matter of when, not if, this research will be able to one day help those who have lost the ability to walk.

Stem Cell Research Should Be Expanded

For these reasons, I'm proud to be a long-term supporter of greater stem cell research. While I was a member of the Illinois Senate, I was the chief cosponsor of the Ronald Reagan Biomedical Research Act, which would specifically permit embryonic stem cell research in Illinois, and establish review of this research by the Illinois Department of Public Health.

And I'm proud to be a cosponsor of the stem cell bill before us today [July 17, 2006]. This bill embodies the innovative thinking that we as a society demand and medical advancement requires. By expanding scientific access to embryonic stem cells which would be otherwise discarded, this bill will help our nation's scientists and researchers develop treatments and cures to help people who suffer from illnesses and injuries for which there are currently none. But the bill is not without limits; it requires that scientific research also be subject to rigorous oversight.

I realize there are moral and ethical issues surrounding this debate. But I also realize that we're not talking about harvesting cells that would've been used to create life and we're not talking about cloning humans. We're talking about using stem cells that would have otherwise been discarded and lost forever—and we're talking about using those stem cells to possibly save the lives of millions of Americans.

Democrats want this bill to pass. Conservative, pro-life Republicans want this bill to pass. By large margins, the American people want this bill to pass. It is only the White House standing in the way of progress—standing in the way of so many potential cures.

I would only ask that the President thinks about this before he picks up his pen to deliver his first veto in six years. I would ask that he thinks about Ryan Schneider and his parents, and all the other families who are sitting and waiting and praying for a cure—hoping that somewhere, a researcher or scientist will find the answer.

The Government Should Fund Stem Cell Research

There was a time in the middle of the last century when America watched helplessly as a mysterious disease left thousands—especially children—disabled for life. The medical community worked tirelessly to try and find a cure, but they needed help—they needed funding to make their research possible.

With a world war raging and the country still emerging from depression, the federal government could have ignored their plight or told them to find a cure on their own.

But that didn't happen. Instead, [President] Franklin Delano Roosevelt helped galvanize a community of compassion and organize the March of Dimes to find the cure for polio. And while Roosevelt knew that his own polio would never be cured by the discovery of a vaccine, he also knew that at its best, government can be used as a force to accomplish together what we cannot achieve on our own.

And so the people began to care and the dimes piled up and the funding started to flow, and fifty years ago, Jonas Salk discovered the polio vaccine.

Americans are looking for that kind of leadership today. All over the country, patients and their families are waiting today for Congress and the President to open the door to the cures of tomorrow. At the dawn of the 21st century, we should approach this research with the same passion and commitment that have led to so many cures and saved so many lives throughout our history.

> **EVALUATING THE AUTHOR'S ARGUMENTS:**
>
> In addition to using facts, statistics, and historical examples, this viewpoint relies on the narrative story of Ryan, a young boy with cerebral palsy whose condition was cured by his own cord stem cells. Did you find this narrative element compelling? Do you think it helped convince you of the author's argument? Why or why not? Explain your answer thoroughly.

The Benefits of Stem Cell Research Have Been Exaggerated

"There are more drawbacks and obstacles to the safe and effective clinical use of embryonic stem cells than once thought."

Richard M. Doerflinger

In the following viewpoint Richard Doerflinger argues that the benefits of stem cell research have been greatly exaggerated. Supporters of stem cell research claim that this biotechnology has the potential to treat and cure diseases that afflict millions of people. However, Doerflinger says that embryonic stem cells have not yet actually provided treatments or cures for any diseases. Embryonic stem cell research is merely in its preliminary phase, and it is too soon to say whether it will prove to be a safe and effective method for treating and curing disease. In fact, Doerflinger claims that in several studies stem cells have caused harmful tumors to grow in animal test subjects. Furthermore, it is extremely complicated to manipulate stem cells and get reliable results. For all of these reasons, Doerflinger concludes that stem

Richard M. Doerflinger, "Testimony Before the Senate Finance Committee, Maryland General Assembly," www.stemcellresearch.org, March 14, 2007.

cell research has been hyped to the public as a cure-all when in reality its promise is unproven and uncertain.

Richard M. Doerflinger is the deputy director of the Secretariat for Pro-Life Activities, a division of the U.S. Conference of Catholic Bishops (USCCB). The USCCB exercises certain pastoral functions on behalf of the Catholic faithful of the United States.

AS YOU READ, CONSIDER THE FOLLOWING QUESTIONS:

1. According to the author, what do stem cells cause over time?
2. Why do people believe stem cells will cure Alzheimer's despite a lack of scientific evidence, according to Doerflinger?
3. What does Doerflinger say is the minimum number of stem cell lines needed for adequate stem cell research? How many are currently available?

I am Richard M. Doerflinger of the Secretariat for Pro-Life Activities, U.S. Conference of Catholic Bishops. I have been invited by the Maryland Catholic Conference to comment on SB [Senate Bill] 59, which would require the state's Stem Cell Research Commission to give priority to embryonic over adult stem cell research.

Currently, the state's stem cell research fund requires that the Commission "gives due consideration to the scientific, medical, and ethical implications of the research." It also urges the Commission to base its review on "the guidelines of the National Institutes of Health [NIH] Center for Scientific Review," which prioritize research in terms of scientific and medical merit. SB 59, then, is based on the proposition that these priorities are unacceptable—that we must, as it were, place our finger on the scale, to give greater weight to stem cell research that is embryonic *regardless* of its scientific, medical or ethical merit. . . .

Embryonic Stem Cells Are Ineffective in Treating Disease

There are more drawbacks and obstacles to the safe and effective clinical use of embryonic stem cells than once thought.

These cells are now known to pose a variety of very serious problems, leading researchers to conclude that "it could be decades before embryonic stem cells cure anything" [as reported in *U.S. News & World Report*, June 6, 2005]. Among the problems:

- The cell lines are difficult to maintain, and they spontaneously develop genetic abnormalities over time—abnormalities closely associated with cancer.

- When placed in animals they form dangerous teratomas (tumors), nullifying their therapeutic goals and often killing

A lab specialist retrieves frozen human embryonic stem cells from a container of liquid nitrogen. Some believe that the benefits of stem cell research are overrated.

the animals. For example, [according to an article in *Somatosensory and Motor Research*] placing cells derived from embryonic stem cells in the injured rat spinal cord "does not improve locomotor recovery and can lead to tumor-like growth of cells, accompanied by increased debilitation, morbidity and mortality." [As written in *Rheumatology*] "Embryonic stem cells injected into the mouse knee joint form teratomas and subsequently destroy the joint."

- Efforts to get these cells to differentiate into functioning cells of one type often fail. Claims that embryonic stem cells had produced functioning pancreatic islet cells were debunked in 2004, when it was found that the cells were only absorbing insulin from their culture medium and releasing it again. Another attempt produced cells that release insulin, but randomly and not in response to their environment. Yet another attempt failed when the cells derived from embryonic stem cells produced tumors in diabetic mice. Commenting on efforts to use embryonic stem cells to create cells for treating diabetes, Douglas Melton of Harvard has said [in the *Wall Street Journal*]: "We are convinced we can do it. We just don't know how."

Stem Cell Research Creates False Hope

Stem cell experts are now urging reduced expectations, fearing a public backlash when patients realize embryonic stem cells were hyped and oversold to them:

- "In order to persuade the public that we must do this work, we often go rather too far in promising what we might achieve . . . I am not entirely convinced that embryonic stem cells will, in my lifetime, and possibly anybody's lifetime for that matter, be holding quite the promise that we desperately hope they will." —Prof. Lord Robert Winston, Gresham Special Lecture, June 20, 2005.

- "The safety issues are high enough that I suspect it will take a long time to get to the clinics, because you don't want to create a disease that's far worse than what you're trying to cure." —Dr. James Thomson of U. of Wisconsin, MSNBC interview, June 25, 2005.

- NIH stem cell expert Ronald McKay, on why many people believe embryonic stem cells will cure Alzheimer's disease despite the scientific consensus that this is extremely unlikely: "To start with, people need a fairy tale." —*Washington Post*, June 10, 2004.

Stem Cell Lines Are Inadequate to Treat Disease

Efforts to solve current problems with embryonic stem cells to develop treatments will require ever broader violations of widely accepted ethical norms.

Supporters cite the RAND Institute's estimate that there are 400,000 "spare" frozen embryos in the U.S., but they ignore the Institute's other conclusions: "Patients have designated only 2.8 percent (about 11,000 embryos) for research. The vast majority of frozen embryos are designated for future attempts at pregnancy. . . . From those embryos designated for research, perhaps as many as 275 stem cell lines (cell cultures suitable for further development) could be created. The actual number is likely to be much lower." This is a woefully inadequate number if any human disease is to be treated.

Two prominent researchers [quoted in the *New York Times*] say that merely determining the "best options for research" (to say nothing of treatments) would require "perhaps 1,000" stem cell lines—about four times as many as are available nationwide. Others say that to reflect the genetic and ethnic diversity of the American population, an embryonic stem cell bank geared toward treating any major disease must include cell lines from many embryos *created solely in order to be destroyed for those cells*—including a disproportionate number of specially created embryos from black couples and other racial minorities, who are underrepresented among fertility clinic clients. Yet another stem cell researcher [quoted in *Scientific American*] says "millions" of embryos from fertility clinics may be needed to create cell lines of sufficient genetic diversity. . . .

The Public Has Been Misled About the Promise of Stem Cell Research

Stem cell research that requires destroying human embryos is unethical, and even more obviously unethical because it cannot live up to the groundless and wildly exaggerated claims that have deceived so many into seeing it as a Holy Grail of miracle cures. At this point, pouring more public funds into this morally problematic and speculative venture can only divert resources and attention away from avenues that offer far more promise for suffering patients and their families. Artificially creating a priority in favor of funding this avenue regardless of medical merit would be grossly irresponsible.

EVALUATING THE AUTHOR'S ARGUMENTS:

Richard Doerflinger quotes from several sources to support the points he makes in his essay. Make a list of everyone he quotes, including their credentials and the nature of their comments. Then, analyze his sources—are they credible? Are they well qualified to speak on the subject?

Alternatives to Embryonic Stem Cell Research Can Cure Disease

Viewpoint 3

David Christensen

"I support stem-cell research that is treating people now —the kind that saves and changes lives without destroying life."

In the following viewpoint David Christensen argues that disease can be treated and cured without doing embryo-based stem cell research. Although it has been touted as a miracle cure, embryonic stem cell research has yet to treat any disease. But Christensen discusses several alternative stem cell treatments that are able to help patients immediately. In fact, Christensen claims that patients with heart disease, spinal-cord injuries, cancer, and sickle-cell anemia have all been successfully treated using either adult stem cells from their own bodies or cord stem cells derived from the blood inside the umbilical cords of newborn babies. Christensen concludes that funding embryonic stem cell research is a waste of money and time and comes with irresolvable ethical problems. He believes the health of Americans would be

David Christensen, "Patients, Not Politics," *National Review*, June 7, 2007. Reproduced by permission.

better served if the government more readily funded alternative stem cell methods instead.

David Christensen is director of congressional affairs at the Family Research Council, a Christian nonprofit think tank and lobbying organization that promotes the traditional family unit based on Judeo-Christian values.

AS YOU READ, CONSIDER THE FOLLOWING QUESTIONS:

1. Who are Doug Rice, Dave Foege, and Jacki Rabon, and what do they all have in common?
2. How much has the government spent on human embryonic stem cell response over the last several years, according to Christensen?
3. What was the success rate of one juvenile diabetes study that treated patients with adult stem cells, as reported by the author?

L iving, breathing people who have been treated by stem cells—some who would have otherwise died—are signs of the great hope of stem-cell research. Take Doug Rice, a bear of a man who was told he had months to live because of heart disease, yet after being treated with his own blood stem cells, his heart function is almost normal. Then there's Dave Foege who also received the same treatment for his ailing heart, after his doctors had sent him home to hospice. And accident victim Jacki Rabon can walk with the aid of braces after she had her own nasal stem cells injected into her spinal-cord injury. Carol Franz is an incredible woman who suffered from multiple myeloma, a bone cancer, until she had her bone-marrow stem cells transplanted. Stephen Sprague has been free from leukemia after having a cord-blood

> **FAST FACT**
>
> Adult stem cells found in bone marrow have been used to treat leukemia, lymphoma, and several inherited blood disorders for over forty years, according to the National Institutes of Health.

stem-cell[1] transplant. And Keone Penn no longer has sickle-cell anemia after receiving a cord-blood stem-cell transplant.

Alternatives to Stem Cell Research Do Not Destroy Embryos

I support stem-cell research that is treating people now—the kind that saves and changes lives without destroying life. The aforementioned did not involve research that requires the destruction of human embryos. The Family Research Council [a Christian nonprofit organization] has opposed embryonic-stem-cell funding bills because they would require taxpayers to fund research that requires human-embryo destruction, and because they are a bait-and-switch. The current bill, S. 5, would fund research on embryos "leftover" from IVF [In Vitro Fertilization] clinics. However, S. 5 would not generate nearly as many stem-cell lines as proponents claim. As Rand [a nonprofit think tank] estimates, leftover embryos could only generate 275 new stem-cell lines because most parents (86 percent) want to use their frozen embryos to have children in the future. S. 5 would actually create an incentive for IVF clinics to generate more "leftover" embryos, and would free up funds for researchers to create and clone embryos with their own finances. Some proponents of S. 5 claim they don't want to create embryos for research.

Cloning Embryos Is Not Ethical Stem Cell Research

But while waiting for the House to debate S. 5, Democratic House leadership on Wednesday [June 6, 2007] brought to the floor a bill (H.R. 2560) by [Colorado representative] Diana DeGette that would do exactly that—create a mass market of cloned human embryos. The bill sanctions the cloning of human embryos for research—so-called "therapeutic cloning"—while prohibiting implantation of cloned embryos into a woman's uterus—so-called "reproductive cloning." This bill is entirely unenforceable and would make cloning human babies more likely, not less. Implanting cloned embryos into a woman would occur in the privacy of the doctor-patient relationship, and once a mother has a clonal pregnancy, what will law enforcement do? In sanctioning cloning embryos for destructive research, this bill encourages

1. Stem cells collected from the blood inside the umbilical cord of newborn babies.

women to sell their eggs to cloning researchers, putting their bodies at risk. South Korean scientists failed to clone human embryos, but did in fact use over 2,000 eggs from over 100 paid women. The De-Gette bill is a debacle. It contains a forfeiture clause that any property used to violate the ban on implantation would become the property of the U.S. government. Does that mean if a woman had a cloned baby, the baby would become government property? Since it also prohibits

Sources of Adult Stem Cells

This chart shows examples of tissues from which adult stem cells have been isolated, as well as some of the derivatives from those stem cells. Adult stem cells have been shown to be effective in treating animal models of disease, including such diseases as diabetes, stroke, spinal cord injury, Parkinson's disease, and retinal degeneration. They are less controversial than embryonic stem cells because no embryo needs to be destroyed. However, it is debated whether they are as useful as embryonic stem cells for curing disease.

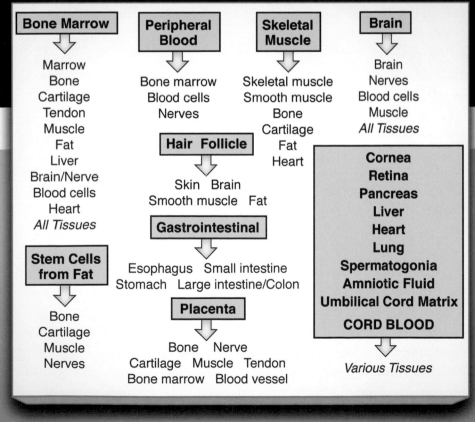

Taken from: David A. Prentice, written testimony for the Mississippi Senate Public Health and Welfare Committee, February 22, 2006. http://stemcellresearch.org/testimony/Prentice-MS-SenateHearing-2006.pdf.

Diana DeGette and Mike Castle, both members of the U.S. House of Representatives, sponsored an embryonic stem cell research bill. Critics say the bill would create a mass market in cloned human embryos.

importing or receiving cloned embryos intended to clone babies, then if any cloned embryo is confiscated would they become government property? The only way to prevent baby cloning is to stop the process at the creation of cloned embryos. This is precisely what Canada, France, and Germany have done. Even the United Nations passed a declaration to ban all human cloning. Thankfully, the DeGette cloning bill was defeated.

Adult Stem Cell Treatments Are Effective Treatments Against Disease

Neither human embryonic-stem-cell research, which the administration has funded to the tune of over $150 million over the past several years, nor human cloning, has treated anyone of any disease. Instead of pouring more money into this therapy-deprived research, we should be expediting stem-cell research that is showing ability to treat not only cancers and blood diseases but is also increasingly helping patients with spinal-cord injury, heart disease, diabetes, and Parkinson's. Two studies, one in the U.K. and one in Kentucky, have shown that Parkinson's symptoms could be reduced by stimulating brain stem cells to produce dopamine. Many patients like Carol, Stephen, and Keone are being treated in the U.S. Unfortunately, many patients like Doug, Dave, and Jacki have had to travel overseas to get an adult-stem-cell treatment even though their stem-cell treatments were pioneered by U.S. researchers. Indeed, a study was just published in which a U.S. scientist used adult stem cells to help 13 of 15 juvenile-diabetes patients. This researcher had to do this clinical trial in Brazil and not in the more restrictive, embryonic-stem cell-fixated U.S. Patients should not have to travel overseas to get an ethical life-saving treatment.

The FDA [Food and Drug Administration] and NIH [National Institutes of Health] need to step up in approving these adult-stem-cell studies. If Congress really wants to help treat patients, instead of just scoring political points, they should pass a bill directing NIH to fund groundbreaking research and clinical trials using stem cells that are treating people. The NIH, led by the evidence-immune Dr. Elias Zerhouni, needs to do a better job of funding adult-stem-cell research with near-term clinical benefits, and the FDA needs to expedite approval of clinical trials here in the U.S. Thankfully, the FDA has approved trials for heart disease in Texas and Maryland, and they finally approved one diabetes trial led by Dr. Denise Faustman at Harvard (though the NIH wouldn't fund it). They need to do better.

Adult Stem Cell Research Requires Federal Funding

A bill prioritizing further stem-cell research with the greatest potential for near-term clinical benefit would bring more therapies to patients now. And full funding for the National Cord Blood Bank is a must. I just spoke with Doug Rice and his heart function is almost normal, thanks to his adult-stem-cell treatment. We could be helping the millions like him here in the U.S. Congress is too busy debating a bill that everyone knows is dead in the water. The president will veto it and Congress does not have the votes to override. Instead of redirecting federal funds away from adult-stem-cell treatments which are increasingly benefiting patients, or trying to promote cloning, we should fully fund the National Cord Blood Bank and direct NIH to increase and prioritize its funding of these adult-stem-cell treatments.

EVALUATING THE AUTHOR'S ARGUMENTS:

In the viewpoint you just read, David Christensen uses history, facts, and examples to make his argument that adult stem cells and other alternative stem cell methods are more effective than embryonic stem cells in treating and curing disease. He does not, however, use any quotations to support his point. If you were to rewrite this article and insert quotations, what authorities might you quote from? Where would you place these quotations to bolster the points Christensen makes?

Alternatives to Embryonic Stem Cell Research Cannot Effectively Cure Disease

Coalition for the Advancement of Medical Research

"Certain, important medical questions can only be examined through embryonic stem cell research."

In the following viewpoint the Coalition for the Advancement of Medical Research (CAMR) argues that embryonic stem cell research is the only path toward answering important medical questions. CAMR points to the importance of pluripotent cells—those that can develop into any cell type—and contends that embryonic research is the best way to explore these pluripotent cells. Alternative methods for creating pluripotency, such as using adult cells, are not as accurate and have safety hazards. CAMR is a bipartisan coalition comprised of more than 100 patient

Coalition for the Advancement of Medical Research, "Stem Cell Research Developments," 2008.

organizations, universities, scientific societies, and foundations. CAMR focuses on developing better treatments and cures for individuals with life-threatening illnesses and disorders.

AS YOU READ, CONSIDER THE FOLLOWING QUESTIONS:

1. What is the iPS method? What are the problems CAMR sees with this method?
2. What is "parthenogenesis"? How is this process different from embryonic stem cell research?
3. How does the Dickey-Wicker amendment affect embryonic stem cell research?

CAMR's ultimate mission is to help end the suffering of the 100 million Americans with diseases and conditions that may someday be treated or even cured through progress in the field of human embryonic stem cell research. CAMR supports all ethical research that unlocks the secrets of pluripotent cells—cells that can develop into any cell type. The world's leading scientists assert that embryonic stem cell research remains the most promising key to demystifying these cells. The recent breakthroughs, while laudable, by no means obviate the need for further embryonic stem cell research. Embryonic stem cell research is more important now than ever.

This fact sheet contains summary descriptions of recent stem cell-related developments that have been in the news. The first, induced pluripotent stem cells (iPS), garnered the most attention as it reprogrammed adult cells to a pluripotent state. The second breakthrough, conducted by a company called Advanced Cell Technology, uses a controversial technique to remove cells from an early-stage embryo. Theoretically, this process does not harm the embryo but further research is needed to understand and effectively replicate this process. Finally, an announcement from the company Stemgen has refocused attention on somatic cell nuclear transfer (SCNT), a technique supported by CAMR. The announcement of any type of breakthrough is the beginning of a long process. Any development will require years of validation before it can reach the stage of progress we now have with human embryonic stem cell research. Scientists and other experts are available for briefings or meetings to provide further details about any of this research.

Induced Pluripotent Stem Cells (iPS)

Dr. James Thomson of the University of Wisconsin and Dr. Shinya Yamanaka of Kyoto University published studies in 2007 that offer a new approach for developing what appear to be pluripotent cells. Similar studies have since been published by researchers at Harvard University. In all of the studies, genes were delivered via a virus agent to an adult cell. The genes reprogram the cell and "turn back the clock"—reverting the cell to a pluripotent state that can be used to generate stem cell lines. Because iPS uses adult cells (one study used discarded tissue from newborn circumcisions) and does not require a human egg or embryo, many assert that this research ends the need for embryonic stem cell research. However, there are several safety concerns about this technique such as the high frequency of tumor development and the hazards associated with using a virus to deliver the genes. Because of this, Thompson, Yamanaka and other scientists continue to see the need for embryonic stem cell research.

In vitro fertilization procedures result in many excess embryos. Proponents say these embryos should be allowed to be donated to scientists for research.

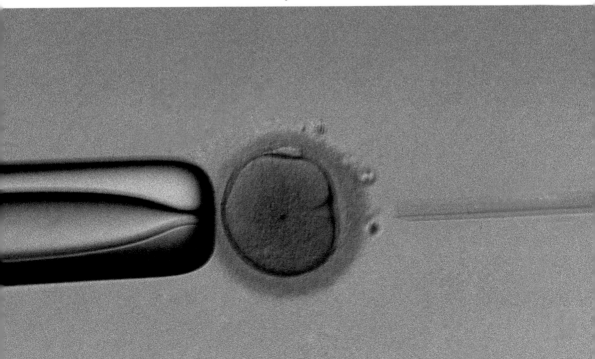

Research Must Continue

Certain, important medical questions can only be examined through embryonic stem cell research. As Dr. George Daley, a member of the Harvard Stem Cell Institute's Executive Committee and President of the International Society for Stem Cell Research has noted, "despite success in generating iPS cells, we are not abandoning our efforts to derive new human stem cell lines by nuclear transfer. We are not yet certain which type of cell will prove most useful for medical applications. Besides, nuclear transfer is an experimental method that asks very important questions that will never be answered by reprogramming skin cells with defined genes."

The iPS discoveries were derivatives of embryonic stem cell research. It is only because embryonic stem cell research was conducted first, that we have iPS now. Dr. Yamanaka has written, ". . . the recent advancements in iPS cell research would not be possible if it were not for the many years of dedicated hES cell research [human embryonic stem cell research] that preceded them. We cannot support the notion that iPS cell research can advance without hES [human embryonic stem] cell

© 2004 Vince O'Farrell, *The Illawarra Mercury*, and PoliticalCartoons.com.

research." (*Cell Stem Cell*, October 2007, coauthored article with Drs. Insoo Hyun, Konrad Hochedlinger, and Rudolf Jaenisch)

There are safety concerns associated with the iPS model. As Dr. Story Landis, chair of the NIH stem cell task force, asserted in public comments at the Parkinson's Action Network Forum (February 2008) one of the "major potential hopes for stem cells is that scientists could use pluripotent stem cells to create tissue replacement therapies for diseases." However, Landis said scientists working on iPS successfully reprogrammed these cells by using viruses to introduce the reprogramming genes, one of which is known to cause cancer, thereby making this method in its current form "absolutely" unsuitable for any kind of transplant. "So while this is a huge scientific step forward, there are many unanswered questions," she said.

We do not know enough about pluripotent cells to know if the iPS versions are identical and it is unlikely that they will behave like exact copies. Dr. Landis stated at the American Health Lawyers Association's (AHLA) annual conference (January 2008), "The game isn't over because we don't actually know that these cells [iPS] are identical to human embryonic stem cells. There are in fact differences," she said. "The likelihood and it is my personal belief, that you end up with something identical to that pristine human embryonic stem cell is about zero. We don't know. It's a very interesting question, and scientists are certainly looking at that." Continued embryonic stem cell research is required to answer those questions. Rather than obviating the need for embryonic stem cell research, iPS provides another testament to the importance of such research.

More work is needed to validate the iPS results. Dr. Kevin Eggan, a leading researcher at Harvard University stated in a *Science* article (February 2008) that "to validate iPS cells, scientists must make huge [numbers] . . . from many different people and compare them in a battery of tests with embryonic stem cells." Validating the results requires moving forward with embryonic stem cell research.

Federal limitations should be overturned and removed. After his iPS announcement, Dr. Thomson asserted in an editorial co-authored by Dr. Alan Leshner (chief executive of the American Association for the Advancement of Science and executive publisher of the journal *Science*) in *The Washington Post* (December 3, 2007) that, "We hope Congress will override the president's veto of the Stem Cell Research Enhancement Act. Further delays in pursuing the clearly viable option of embryonic stem cells will result in an irretrievable loss of time, especially if the new approach fails to prove itself."

All avenues of research should be pursued. Writing in the journal *Cell Stem Cell*, Drs. Yamanaka, Konrad Hochedlinger (Harvard Stem Cell Institute's Principal Investigator) and Rudolf Jaenisch (MIT's Whitehead Institute) assert that "We hold that research into all avenues of human stem cell research must proceed together. Society deserves to have the full commitment of scientific inquiry at its service. And science is a practice that works best when it is approached with an open and creative mind. Research into one approach can inspire new ideas in unpredictable and exciting ways."

Dr. Landis' comments at the AHLA conference further bolster this position: "We simply don't know where the advances are going to come from for any particular disease, and as an institute director, we're responsible for 600 diseases, common diseases, rare diseases, and to say that all the answers to neurogenerative diseases are going to come from adult stem cells or reprogrammed stem cells, I think that's just unreasonable."

The iPS discoveries were possible only because embryonic stem cell research was conducted first. Dr. Yamanaka has written, ". . . the recent advancements in iPS cell research would not be possible if it were not for the many years of dedicated hES cell research [embryonic stem cell research] that preceded them. We cannot support the notion that iPS cell research can advance without hES [embryonic stem] cell research." (*Cell Stem Cell*, October 2007, coauthored article with Drs. Insoo Hyun, Konrad Hochedlinger, and Rudolf Jaenisch)

Advanced Cell Technology

In January 2008, a published study in the journal *Cell Stem Cell* announced that Advanced Cell Technology (ACT), a private company, created a pluripotent stem cell line from a single cell removed from an early stage embryo without causing harm to the embryo. This process of inducing a single cell to replicate is sometimes called "parthenogenesis." The technique of removing an embryonic cell from a blastocyst prior to implantation is often used in fertility clinics for pre-implantation genetic testing and is controversial. While now growing in use and acceptance, the long-term effects of removing the single cell from an embryo prior to implantation are not known nor fully understood. Further research is needed to answer safety questions regarding this procedure.

Concerns About the ACT Study

The results from the ACT study have not been replicated elsewhere. ACT is a privately held company and aspects of its work are not publicly available for scrutiny.

The "Dickey-Wicker" amendment that has been included in the Labor-Health and Human Services-Education Appropriations bill for the past several years severely limits research and experimentation on human embryos. This has prevented federally funded scientists from doing the long-term studies needed to confirm the safety of the technique.

Therapeutic Cloning (SCNT)

In January 2008, private company Stemagen announced it had successfully performed a technique called somatic cell nuclear transfer (SCNT), otherwise known as therapeutic cloning, on human cells. Stemagen is the first company to announce that it successfully performed SCNT on human cells. In this process an unfertilized human egg cell (oocyte) is used to develop pluripotent stem cell lines. The genetic material is removed from the egg, and genetic material from a donor is placed in the egg. Scientists are able to induce cellular division and create pluripotent stem cells. These stem cells are a perfect match to the genetic donor and have the potential to be used for a variety of treatments. CAMR fully supports SCNT and joins with the entire scientific and ethics communities in opposing human cloning, also called reproductive cloning.

Therapeutic cloning (SCNT) continues to be a valid and important avenue to pursue in the field of stem cell research and must remain a legal option for scientists. Human reproductive cloning is not supported by any ethical group or scientist. CAMR strongly supports efforts to ban human reproductive cloning by banning implantation of blastocysts created by SCNT. CAMR does not support overly broad bans that would also prohibit SCNT research.

CAMR Supports All Ethical Research

CAMR supports all ethical research that will help end the suffering of the more than 100 million Americans with diseases and conditions that may someday be treated or even cured through progress in the field of embryonic stem cell research.

Embryonic stem cell research remains the most promising avenue of research to cure diseases and end suffering.

Other avenues of study, including iPS, are very new and will require years of validation before they can reach the stage of progress we now have with embryonic stem cell research. Too many patients and their families are suffering and we must not abandon the important work done to date with embryonic stem cell lines. While CAMR supports all ethical research, it is imperative that the Stem Cell Research Enhancement Act (S.5), or similar legislation, be enacted, and the federal barriers to full funding for embryonic stem cell research be removed.

EVALUATING THE AUTHOR'S ARGUMENTS:

CAMR believes that the alternatives to embryonic stem cell research outlined in this viewpoint are not promising enough to justify discontinuing the research. Based on what you have read in this viewpoint, do you think the argument is adequately supported? Explain your answer.

Stem Cells Made from Skin Are Effective

Bernadine Healy

"Stem cells can be made better, cheaper, and faster from skin than from embryos."

In the following viewpoint Bernadine Healy argues that stem cells made from skin are an effective way to treat disease. She claims that adult stem cells can be harvested from a person's skin and transformed into other types of cells, including heart, liver, and nerve cells. These cells could be used to replace that person's damaged cells, tissues, and organs. Healy explains these kinds of stem cells are effective because they contain the same DNA of the person who donated the skin and are thus easily programmable. The benefit of this type of stem cell research is that it does not require the destruction of human embryos, nor does it rely upon egg donations. Furthermore, Healy explains that this technique is easier and faster than embryonic stem cell research. Healy concludes that stem cell research from skin can reduce the controversy and risks associated with embryonic stem cell research.

Bernadine Healy is health editor for *U.S. News & World Report* and writes the "On Health" column. She is a member of the President's Council of Advisors on Science and Technology and has served as director of the National Institutes of Health and president and CEO of the American Red Cross.

AS YOU READ, CONSIDER THE FOLLOWING QUESTIONS:

1. According to the author, stem cells made from skin mimic what type of stem cells?
2. What discovery does the author say paved the way for stem cells to be created without embryos?
3. What does the author mean when she says that stem cells made from skin can be used to "personalize medicine"?

The new year [2008] opens with one of the greatest breakthroughs in medical science since [scientist] Ian Wilmut used cells from an adult sheep to clone Dolly the lamb in 1996. Human stem cells, which for all intents and purposes are identical to the highly prized but controversial ones harvested from human embryos, now can be made from adult skin, without using embryos or eggs. Separate research groups headed by Shinya Yamanaka of [Japan's] Kyoto University and James Thomson of the University of Wisconsin unveiled the technique in late November [2007]. A third group, from Harvard, confirmed that work barely a month later. It seems the path to curing diseases like diabetes, Parkinson's, and many inherited disorders has a shortcut. In fact, stem cell pioneer Rudolf Jaenisch of the Whitehead Institute in Cambridge, Mass., just showed that a mouse version of these cells cures mice with sickle cell anemia.

Skin Stem Cells Mimic Embryonic Stem Cells

Known by the rather clunky name "induced pluripotent stem [iPS] cells," the new creations look and behave like embryonic stem cells taken from seven-day-old embryos; both are able to turn into any type of cell in the body—skin, heart, liver, nerve, you name it. Even better, iPS cells' DNA matches that of the person who provides the skin, which is crucial if the cells are to be used to replace that person's own destroyed or damaged tissue. To date, intense efforts in the United States and around the world to make such genetically matched stem cells through cloning, an alternative approach, have failed miserably.

Adult Stem Cells Are Easily Programmable

Even cloning of an animal embryo, like the one that led to Dolly, is a laborious process involving "nuclear transfer," in which an adult

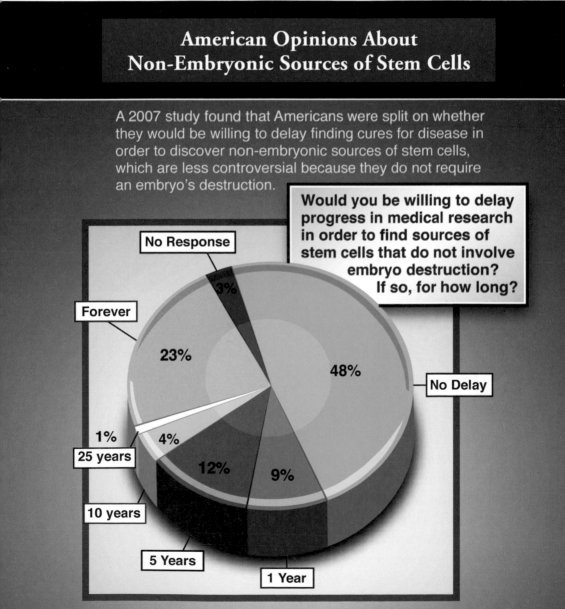

American Opinions About Non-Embryonic Sources of Stem Cells

A 2007 study found that Americans were split on whether they would be willing to delay finding cures for disease in order to discover non-embryonic sources of stem cells, which are less controversial because they do not require an embryo's destruction.

Would you be willing to delay progress in medical research in order to find sources of stem cells that do not involve embryo destruction? If so, for how long?

No Response 3%

Forever 23%

48% No Delay

1% 25 years

4%

12% 9%

10 years

5 Years

1 Year

Taken from: Kathy L. Hudson, Joan Scott, and Ruth Faden, "Values in Conflict: Public Attitudes on Embryonic Stem Cell Research," Genetics and Public Policy Center, October 2005. www.dnapolicy.org/images/reportpdfs/2005ValuesInConflict.pdf.

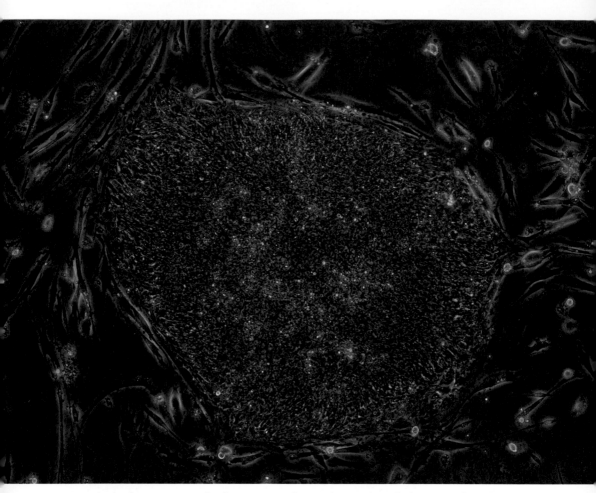

Hundreds of sperm race to fertilize an ovum during the creation of a human embryo for stem cell research. The nuclear transfer process will destroy the embryo, leading to ethical challenges.

cell's nucleus and its payload of DNA are teased out and placed into a donated unfertilized egg that has been stripped of its own DNA. In a small fraction of transfers, the egg almost magically reprograms the adult nucleus to orchestrate the development of an embryo—as if it were in a fertilized egg. Cloning embryos from adult animals has been successful in many species other than sheep, including cows, cats, pigs, and mice. But as one ascends the evolutionary tree, this gets more difficult. Only last year, the first-ever primate stem cells were made from a cloned monkey embryo.

Difficulties aside, making human stem cells by nuclear transfer invariably requires creating and destroying a human embryo, which raises ethical issues. But the broader lesson of Dolly—that DNA from adults can be reprogrammed to an earlier stage of development— paved the way for making stem cells without embryos. In this new approach, inserted genes reprogram an adult cell directly. To do this, scientists needed to know the many genes that are active in stem cells and are turned off as cells mature. What's so remarkable is that only three or four inserted genes accomplish the transformation.

Stem Cells Made from Skin Spare Embryos

Although Dolly laid the intellectual groundwork, Wilmut says the feat of creating iPS cells may be more important than his own because it's so practical. The technique not only spares embryos; it doesn't even use eggs. Extracting eggs from young women volunteers brings ethical and medical concerns of its own that even now limit research. Also, gene-driven reprogramming is easier and faster and could be adapted to routine clinical use. As Wilmut says, a researcher can "sprinkle stardust on cells in a dish" and return three weeks later to find colonies of embryonic-like stem cells. Sure, there are hurdles. Many thousands of cells get "sprinkled" for each one that transforms. And the virus that carries genes into the cells, or the gene reprogramming itself, could be risky to humans. But most scientists I've spoken with predict these problems are not insurmountable.

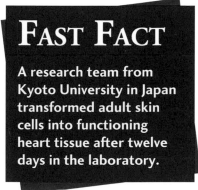

FAST FACT

A research team from Kyoto University in Japan transformed adult skin cells into functioning heart tissue after twelve days in the laboratory.

Stem Cells Made from Skin Can Be Used to Treat Disease

Meanwhile, in an immediate windfall, scientists can put human disease in a test tube by having patients serve up a bit of skin. From that, researchers will be able to generate an unlimited supply of specialized cells prone to a particular disease and get an idea, for example, of how different patients respond to certain drugs. This brings a whole new dimension to personalized medicine.

Since the initial exuberant response to iPS, some have been pouring cold water on the discovery, fearing that embryo work will be deserted. But embryo-derived cell lines will remain the gold standard for a while; it's too early to hold a beauty contest. Yet if stem cells can be made better, cheaper, and faster from skin than from embryos, that's no cause for hand-wringing. It would be a stem cell victory like no other.

EVALUATING THE AUTHORS' ARGUMENTS:

In this viewpoint Bernadine Healy explains that stem cells made from adult skin can be used to treat disease effectively. The author of the following viewpoint, Sharon Begley, says that stem cells made from skin have been overhyped and can only be used to study disease, not treat it. With which author's perspective do you agree? Why?

Stem Cells Made from Skin Are Not Effective

Sharon Begley

"The new method for creating stem cells is unlikely to lead to treatments and cures any sooner than having only the old one."

In the following viewpoint Sharon Begley argues that adult stem cells made from skin cannot be used to treat or cure disease. While scientists have been able to reprogram adult skin cells to become stem cells, these cells are unreliable and do not offer cures for devastating diseases like Parkinson's. In fact, Begley explains that these reprogrammed cells require a gene that has a tendency to trigger, and in some cases cause, cancer. As such, these cells will not be suitable for use in transplant therapies. Furthermore, Begley explains, they will not replace the need for embryonic stem cells to provide cures for debilitating diseases. Instead these adult stem cells will merely be used to study new therapies that will one day help treat disease, the author concludes.

Sharon Begley has been a senior editor with *Newsweek* since 1996 and has been a senior writer for *Newsweek*'s science stories since January 1990.

AS YOU READ, CONSIDER THE FOLLOWING QUESTIONS:

1. According to the author, manipulating adult stem cells has worked in only what two animals?
2. One of the four genes used in adult stem cells made from skin can trigger what disease, according to the author?
3. What does the author say is "more fiction than fact"?

S o skin cells can turn into stem cells. That doesn't mean cures are in sight.

When President George W. Bush vetoed Congress's latest stem-cell bill in June [2007] he tried to soften the blow and minimize the political damage by arguing science, not politics. Sources of stem cells other than days-old human embryos, he said, offered just as much promise for understanding and treating disease. Bush, it turns out, was well briefed. Earlier this year [2007] scientists in Kyoto had announced a feat of biological legerdemain that promised to obviate the long and bitter stem-cell debate, which has pitted the moral status of days-old human embryos against the moral duty of biomedical researchers and society to seek cures for devastating diseases. The Kyoto University team had taken skin cells from adult mice and "reprogrammed" them, turning back the biological calendar so the adult cells could, like embryonic cells, turn into any kind of cell in the body. Bush knew from his advisers that labs were close to accomplishing that with human cells, too.

Stem Cells Made from Skin Only a Tool to Study Disease

Now the Kyoto scientists and a team from the University of Wisconsin–Madison have in fact done it. The groups independently announced last week that they had taken a quartet of human genes, slipped them into adult skin cells, and thereby reprogrammed the cells to become stem cells. But although the feat is being hailed as eliminating the need to produce—let alone destroy—embryos as a source of stem cells, it doesn't. And the attention the discovery is receiving obscures an important change in stem-cell science. While the research was once hailed as leading directly to cures—by turning stem cells into neuronal cells that could be implanted in patients with Parkinson's disease, say—it now looks like something much more mundane: another laboratory tool to study different diseases, yielding insights that would launch the slow, years-long search for new therapies. "It's likely that studying human disease is on a faster track

Kyoto University professor Shinya Yamanaka (pictured) takes the view that reprogramming stem cells in lieu of using embryonic stem cells is a serious research mistake.

Existing Stem Cell Lines

The following human embryonic stem cell lines are eligible for use in federal research, according to U.S. policy. Although 78 lines are eligible, only 22 are actually available or viable to be used for research.

Name	Number of stem cell lines	
	Eligible	Available
BresaGen, Inc., Athens, GA	4	3
Cell & Gene Therapy Institute (Pochon CHA University), Seoul, Korea	2	
Cellaritis AB, Goteborg, Sweden	3	2
CyThera, Inc., San Diego, CA	9	0
ES Cell International, Melbourne, Australia	6	6
Geron Corporation, Menlo Park, CA	7	
Goteborg University, Goteborg, Sweden	16	
Karolinska Institute, Stockholm, Sweden	6	0
Maria Biotech Co. Ltd. – Maria Infertility Hospital Medical Institute, Seoul, Korea	3	
MizMedi Hospital – Seoul National University, Seoul, Korea	1	1
National Center for Biological Sciences/Tata Institute of Fundamental Research, Bangalore, India	3	
Reliance Life Sciences, Mumbai, India	7	
Technion University, Haifa, Israel	4	3
University of California, San Francisco, CA	2	2
Wisconsin Alumni Research Foundation, Madison, WI	5	5
Total	78	22

Taken from: Judith A. Johnson, "Stem Cell Research," CRS Report for Congress, January 11, 2006.

than using stem cells for transplant therapy," says Fred Gage of the Salk Institute. For that purpose, having the new method for creating stem cells is unlikely to lead to treatments and cures any sooner than having only the old one.

Adult Stem Cells Can Cause Disease

The magic of embryonic stem cells comes from the fact that, like a newborn baby, no life path has been closed to them. They can mature into a muscle cell or a liver cell or any other. Although adult cells contain the same genes as embryonic cells, most of their genes have been silenced. One way to make all the genes sing again is to inject them into an egg. Something in the goopy ovoid returns the genes to their embryonic state, allowing the egg to develop into a ball of stem cells. This approach has worked in mice and monkeys, but not humans. The Kyoto and Wisconsin scientists discovered another way to produce human stem cells: use a virus to ferry four human genes into an adult cell. The quartet reprograms the cell back to its embryonic state of unlimited potential.

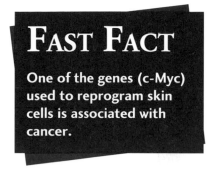

FAST FACT

One of the genes (c-Myc) used to reprogram skin cells is associated with cancer.

If this recipe works reliably, notes the journal *Science*, which published the Wisconsin study, we "would not need human embryos or [eggs] to generate patient-specific stem cells—and therefore could bypass the ethical and political debates that have surrounded the field." But that's a big "if." For one thing, the virus used to carry the four genes has a bad habit of plunking itself into spots on a cell's chromosomes where it can trigger cancer. Also, one of the four genes is itself a cancer-causing gene. Malignant cells are unlikely to be very useful for either basic research or as transplants, says Konrad Hochedlinger of Massachusetts General Hospital.

Adult Stem Cells Do Not Eliminate the Need for Embryonic Stem Cells

But that's not why Kyoto's Shinya Yamanaka and colleagues call the claim that reprogrammed stem cells eliminate the need for embryonic stem cells "a serious mistake." For one thing, it will be years before scientists understand reprogrammed stem cells—how to get them to mature into different tissues, for instance. Also, embryonic stem cells will be needed as a benchmark, something to compare to the power of reprogrammed stem cells to treat disease (which embryonic stem cells have done in lab animals). "Applications of stem-cell science would be indefensibly delayed if [research on reprogrammed stem cells] is pursued at the expense of further human embryonic stem-cell research," Yamanaka and colleagues wrote last month.

Stem Cells Made from Skin Cannot Cure Disease

To a public for whom stem cells equal cure, the real blow will be the realization that the simplistic picture—take a patient's genes, slip them into an egg, let the egg grow and divide into stem cells that are perfect genetic matches for the patient and transplant those cells to treat diabetes, Parkinson's, Alzheimer's—is more fiction than fact. "Creating cell lines for transplant is unlikely to come down the pike any time soon," Paul Nurse, president of Rockefeller University and a Nobelist in medicine, told the New York Stem Cell Foundation conference last month [November 2007]. "Opponents [of embryonic stem-cell research] recognized that this was an overselling of the technology." Instead of yielding cures directly, stem cells—reprogrammed and embryonic alike—will take their place alongside other lab systems for studying disease. They will reveal hitherto-unknown causes and pathways of illness, even pointing the way to new drugs. The typical time between such a discovery and a new drug is at least 15 years.

> **EVALUATING THE AUTHOR'S ARGUMENTS:**
>
> Sharon Begley argues that stem cells made from skin do not directly cure disease, but rather can be used as tools to study diseases. In your opinion, does this distinction lessen the importance of the discovery? Or is it still an important discovery? Explain your answer thoroughly.

President George W. Bush has prevented federal funds from being used to support embryonic stem cell research, saying the research crosses a moral boundary.

Government Should Fund Stem Cell Research

> *"Thoughtfully regulated federal funding... would be the best way to ensure that stem cell research fulfills its potential."*

Julie Hutto

In the following viewpoint Julie Hutto argues that the government should fund and support stem cell research. She complains that despite the fact that a majority of Americans approve of embryonic stem cell research, the government has severely limited funding for research to a few existing stem cell lines. According to Hutto this action has prematurely halted the discovery of potentially lifesaving treatments because the available stem cell lines have proved inadequate for vigorous research. She calls on the government to provide scientists and researchers with funding so that new stem cell lines can be developed. In addition, federal funding would help the government develop strict guidelines that hold all research companies and institutions publicly accountable to a standard set of ethical procedures. The author concludes that

Julie Hutto, "Embryonic Stem Cell Research: A Renewed Call for Robust Federal Support," Progressive Policy Institute, June 2, 2005. www.ppionline.org. Reproduced by permission.

government funding of stem cell research will create a comprehensive and regulated program that will ultimately save lives.

Julie Hutto is a master's candidate at the Johns Hopkins University's School of Advanced International Studies and a former research assistant for the Technology and New Economy Project at the Progressive Policy Institute, a nonprofit research and education organization.

AS YOU READ, CONSIDER THE FOLLOWING QUESTIONS:

1. What is the Dickey Amendment, as described by the author?
2. According to the author, what contaminant is found in currently available stem cell lines?
3. Describe the stem cell research efforts the author says are underway in Great Britain and South Korea.

I t is time to admit that the president's four-year-old stem cell policy experiment has failed, and the damage must be undone. In the summer of 2001, [President George W.] Bush decided to limit federal funding for potentially life-saving medical research on embryonic stem cells to a few existing lines of cells. Today [2005], the results of that policy are painfully clear: Federally funded research on the approved lines remains anemic, because the lines have proven to be inadequate for robust studies. Meanwhile, medical researchers in other countries are regularly making international headlines with new breakthroughs.

Easing Federal Funding Restrictions

The administration and most Republicans in Congress are standing against the opinion of a solid majority of Americans, including many in their own party. A May 2005 CBS News survey found that 58 percent of Americans approve of medical research on embryonic stem cells. Another May 2005 survey by CNN/Gallup/USA found that 53 percent specifically support easing the current restrictions on federal funding. Furthermore, Mike Castle (R-Del.) joined Diana DeGette (D-Colo.) in sponsoring the Stem Cell Research Enhancement Act—and a number of anti-abortion Republican legislators, including Sens. Orrin Hatch (R-Utah) and Trent Lott (R-Miss.), and Reps. Joe Barton (R-Texas) and Jo Ann Emerson (R-Mo.), also support the bill. . . .

The Stem Cell Research Enhancement Act is actually modest in its scope. It would simply overturn the president's ban, expanding federally funded stem cell research to stem cell lines created after his arbitrary cut-off date of August 9, 2001. The currently allowable lines are grossly inadequate to support research, so the ban has drastically slowed the advance of breakthrough medical treatments that could potentially alleviate or even cure chronic and lethal conditions that afflict nearly 130 million Americans. The legislation also contains key provisions to reaffirm oversight by the National Institutes of Health (NIH), mandate embryo donor consent, and prohibit payment for donations. It does

State and private funding for stem cell research has led to several breakthroughs. The Harvard Stem Cell Institute derived seventeen new embryonic stem cell lines for research in 2004.

not, however, open federal money for actually creating new stem cell lines from human embryos. That has been prohibited since the early 1990s when Congress first passed the so-called Dickey amendment, an annual rider to the Health and Human Services appropriations bill that bans the use of federal money for any research that harms human embryos, or knowingly subjects them to risks greater than those allowed on fetuses in utero. . . .

Current Stem Cell Lines Are Inadequate

The basic case for federally funded research on embryonic stem cells is the same today as it was in 2001, when PPI [Progressive Policy Institute] released a detailed report on the issue. But developments in the past four years have further underscored the need for it. For instance, under current policy, only 21 stem cell lines are eligible for federally funded research, a fraction of the 60 to 80 lines President Bush said would be available when he announced his policy. But hundreds of lines are needed for genetically diverse research. Worse yet, since President Bush's 2001 declaration, scientists have determined that they cannot use any of the allowable lines in clinical trials or to find cures to human diseases, because the lines are contaminated with mouse feeder cells. This is because in the past scientists included layers of mouse cells, also known as feeder layers, in the petri dishes where they grew stem cell lines. These cells, however, can contain viruses and toxic proteins. A human patient's immune system would reject an organ created from contaminated stem cells if it had antibodies from these latent viruses. Some newer, privately derived stem cell lines are free of mouse cell contamination but scientists cannot use federal funds to study these.

State and Private Funding Are Not Adequate Substitutes

Several states, most recently Connecticut and Massachusetts, have responded to the federal funding deficit with their own legislation and funds for stem cell research. In a November 2004 referendum, California pledged $3 billion for stem cell research over the next decade. Acting New Jersey Gov. Richard Codey also announced robust funding for stem cell research ($380 million), but budget shortfalls have held up the funds. In addition, Illinois, Maryland, New York, Texas, and Wisconsin are all considering legislation that either pledges funding for stem cell research or expresses support for the research. Meanwhile, legislation under consideration in Hawaii and North Carolina would fund studies into whether or not to support stem cell research there.

Some private donors have also tried to fill the federal funding deficit, and such funding has led to several breakthroughs in the past few years. The Harvard Stem Cell Institute, for instance, derived 17 new embryonic stem cell lines in March 2004. Later that year, a Chicago fertility clinic produced 12 additional lines. However, private funding for stem cell research is limited because it is still in the most basic stages, and pharmaceutical companies view the research as too risky and the benefits too far off.

With Federal Funding Comes Rigorous Oversight

While state and private funding for stem cell research provide tangible evidence of Americans' support for the research, the patchwork of private and state-funded efforts is a second-rate solution to the federal funding gap for several reasons. First, to limit federally funded research but allow unfettered private and state-funded research slows the search for cures but does not prevent the destruction of embryos. A partial ban also falls disproportionately on academic scientists, who rely heavily on NIH grants for their research. Second, federally funded stem cell research falls under the auspices of NIH ethical guidelines, so it is subject to the most transparent, public, and rigorous oversight. NIH requires that scientists only use federal funds for research on stem cell lines derived from embryos donated for IVF, a guideline that is reiterated in the new House bill, but that policy may not hold in a state-by-state system. Moreover, proposals funded under these guidelines are publicly accountable and represent the best possible consensus on this research because they have been thoroughly vetted and submitted for public comment. Additionally, because federally funded stem cell research follows NIH guidelines, expanding it helps to ensure that the United States can take the lead in shaping international research ethics.

The United States Needs Federal Funding to Compete with International Stem Cell Research

The dogged inflexibility of the president and his Republican allies also threatens America's global leadership on medical research and biotechnology. As they have dug in their heels, several other countries, notably Great Britain and South Korea, have greatly increased governmental funding for stem cell research in the past few years. The British government not only funds research on stem cell lines derived through private funds, it directly funds the derivation of new lines. One of the latest British initiatives was a $30 million commitment to stem cell research at Cambridge University. Similarly, unlike in the United States, stem cell research in South Korea has the explicit backing of the president and has received $27 million in funding from the South Korean government since 2002. South Korean scientists have since leapt forward by cloning human embryos, extracting embryonic stem cells from

© M.e. Cohen, Humorlink.com, and PoliticalCartoons.com.

them, and showing that these cells can be made to grow into different body tissues, a process known as therapeutic cloning. (That process may eventually lead to organ transplants in which the organs are grown from the patients' own cells, which could avoid the grave risk of patients rejecting donated organs.) In May 2005, the same research team, financed by the South Korean government, trumpeted their own breakthrough when they discovered a more efficient method to derive stem cell lines. Using this method, they successfully created stem cell lines that were genetic matches for nine patients of varying ages. While Bush's 2001 edict has not yet been followed by a major exodus of top stem cell researchers out of the United States, in the future more may choose, as noted scientist Roger Pederson already has, to move to countries that are aggressively pursuing stem cell research.

"Fulfilling Its Potential"

Scientists around the world are increasingly excited about the prospects that stem cell research could yield new treatments and cures for myriad chronic diseases. Progressives in the United States should support them in their research efforts. Thoughtfully regulated federal funding under the auspices of NIH guidelines—as the Stem Cell Research Enhancement Act proposes—would be the best way to ensure that stem cell research fulfills its potential.

> ### EVALUATING THE AUTHOR'S ARGUMENTS:
>
> In the viewpoint you just read, Julie Hutto describes how government funding restrictions have severely limited vital stem cell research. Consider the reasons offered for why the government has imposed these restrictions. Do you agree with these reasons? Or do you believe that the government should expand its stem cell research program? Use evidence from the text in your answer.

The Government Should Not Fund Stem Cell Research

Steve Lonegan

"The so-called Stem Cell Research Bond Act is nothing more than an old-fashioned, big-government boondoggle."

In the following viewpoint Steve Lonegan argues against government-sponsored stem cell research. The success of embryonic stem cell research has been speculative at best, the author claims. If stem cell research held the promise that supporters claim it does, then the private sector would be more than willing to fund it. But so far, the private sector has been slow to invest because it is not all that promising a technology. If private investors are reluctant, the author reasons that the government should be wary, too. Furthermore, the author argues that state governments like New Jersey are already in financial trouble and cannot afford to pour money into a less-than-promising endeavor. If the government cannot afford it, then the cost of stem cell research programs will likely fall on taxpayers, who are already strapped in

Steve Lonegan, "Don't Buy the Hype on Stem Cell," *The Record* (Bergen County), October 2007. Reproduced by permission.

these fiscally trying times. For all of these reasons, Lonegan concludes that the government should not be responsible for paying for medical research until it shows some promise of success.

Steve Lonegan is the former mayor of Bogota, New Jersey. He is currently executive director of Americans for Prosperity, an organization of grassroots leaders dedicated to educating citizens about economic policy and mobilizing those citizens as advocates in the public policy process.

AS YOU READ, CONSIDER THE FOLLOWING QUESTIONS:

1. What does the phrase "corporate welfare" mean in the context of this viewpoint?
2. How much does the author estimate funding for embryonic stem cell research would cost a state like New Jersey?
3. How is funding for stem cell research likely to be allocated, according to the author?

It's easy to get caught in the debate over stem cell research as a social issue, connected to abortion, religion and the broad philosophical question of when life begins. When it comes to Question No. 2, however, the philosophical debate, whatever your view, is simply a distraction. Because whether or not you support embryonic stem cell research, the so-called Stem Cell Research Bond Act is nothing more than an old-fashioned, big-government boondoggle.

Stem Cell Research Is Merely Speculative

The act amounts to corporate welfare for the biomedical industry, hundreds of millions of dollars in wasteful spending, and a certain tax hike. With state indebtedness at unsustainable levels, piling on more debt to fund this boondoggle will only exacerbate the state's fiscal stress, without any of the miracle cures we've been promised.

At more than $33 billion, New Jersey is the fourth most indebted state in the nation and is suffering from a stagnant private sector economy. We cannot afford more debt and spending. Adding another $450 million in debt to roll the dice on speculative medical research hardly seems like a smart bet.

Private Investors Should Fund Stem Cell Research

Proponents of the measure point out that the state could reap royalty revenue if there is a major breakthrough, but the likelihood of that happening is remote. If this research were truly promising, there would be no shortage of private sector investors lined up to put their money to work. We are awash in risk capital in this country.

For the state to step in and gamble on something so wildly speculative that there are virtually no takers in the private sector would be a grave mistake. Debt service already consumes a whopping 10 percent (about $3 billion) of our state budget.

Where would the $450 million go? The act has a dangerously expansive definition of "qualified research institutions." It includes not

Federal Funding for Stem Cell Research (in Millions)

The federal government has restricted the amount of funding it will give to embryonic stem cell research because such research requires an embryo to be destroyed. Funds for other types of stem cell research have no such restrictions.

Year	Embryonic Stem Cell Research	Non-Embryonic Stem Cell Research	All Stem Cell Research
2003	133	383	517
2004	113	439	553
2005	137	472	609
2006	148	495	643
2007	147	494	641
2008	146	492	639

Taken from: Jonathan Moreno, Sam Berger, and Alix Rogers, "Divided We Fall: The Need for National Stem Cell Funding," Center for American Progress, April 2007, p. 3.

just universities and other nonprofits engaged in medical research, but also state and local government agencies— so you can bet a portion of the money will be spread around to line the pockets of political cronies.

The simple fact that this statute says local governments can apply for research grants demonstrates either the incompetence of the act's authors or a plan to have political entities like Newark and Camden [cities in New Jersey] receive these "grants" and attempt to embark into "research." Given their failure to manage government services effectively, combined with a history of rampant corruption, this falls nothing short of being absurd.

The act also allows for-profit entities to gorge on these taxpayer funds, providing they enter into a "collaborative agreement" with a nonprofit entity. Of course, most major corporations already have affiliated nonprofit foundations for such a purpose. This will be a major corporate welfare giveaway to fund medical research that free markets have determined has little promise.

Funding Stem Cell Research Will Increase Property Taxes

Who pays for this largesse? New Jersey taxpayers, of course. If the state is unable to meet the interest and principal payments out of existing tax revenues, approval of the ballot question empowers the state to levy a new property tax on every property owner in the state, in essence using our homes and businesses as collateral to secure these bonds.

If that is not enough, the state can also establish a tax on our personal property. Given the Legislature's recent track record on raising taxes versus cutting spending, it's a near certainty this automatic tax hike would take effect to pay for the costs of the act.

Supporters contend that "an independent research review panel" and an "independent ethics review panel" will impartially and ethically choose research projects, but this is nothing more than a smoke-

Acting New Jersey governor Richard J. Codey rehearses a speech in which he will discuss his state's involvement in stem cell research.

screen. Does anyone really think that this panel will be made up of anything but political hacks?

Stem Cell Research Holds Little Promise in Curing Disease

The fact that the private sector seems largely uninterested in embryonic stem cell research, which has to date yielded not a single promising new cure or treatment, should be taken as powerful evidence that this area of research carries considerably less promise than its backers in the political class believe.

The moral questions implicated by stem cell research are complex and emotional. But the fiscal issues involved in this ballot question couldn't be simpler.

This is a $450 million giveaway to political insiders and favored medical companies at taxpayer expense, all wrapped up in feel-good politics.

EVALUATING THE AUTHOR'S ARGUMENTS:

Steve Lonegan characterizes supporters of government-sponsored stem cell research as "political cronies" and "political hacks." In your opinion, do such characterizations strengthen or weaken his argument? Did they make his ideas more interesting to read, or did you feel they detracted from his points? Explain your reasoning.

State Governments Will Fund Stem Cell Research If the Federal Government Does Not

"Federal funding restrictions have provoked an outpouring of state initiatives for research funding for stem-cell research."

Ronald Bailey

In the following viewpoint Ronald Bailey discusses the fact that although the government has restricted federal funding for stem cell research, many states are willing to fund it. Indeed, the lack of federal funding has spurred many states to invest in their own state-sponsored stem cell research programs. As a result, California, New Jersey, Connecticut, and Illinois have already contributed millions of dollars to stem cell research in their states, and several others are considering whether to fund the research. Some states are financing

Ronald Bailey, "Do We Really Need the Feds?" *Reason*, August 24, 2005. Reproduced by permission of *Reason* magazine and Reason.com.

these programs with bonds, while others have come up with unique funding methods, such as using taxes from cosmetic procedures or dipping into state tobacco settlement proceeds. As a result, these states are seeing an increase in jobs, funding, and prestige, all of which are beneficial. The author concludes by saying that given several states' support of stem cell research, federal funding may no longer be necessary—and in fact, the state-funded efforts may produce better results than had the federal government chosen to fund stem cell research in the first place.

Ronald Bailey is an award-winning science correspondent for *Reason* magazine and Reason.com, where he writes a weekly science and technology column. Bailey is also the author of the book *Liberation Biology: The Moral and Scientific Case for the Biotech Revolution.*

AS YOU READ, CONSIDER THE FOLLOWING QUESTIONS:

1. What reason did President George W. Bush give for restricting federal funding of stem cell research, as reported by Bailey?
2. Which four states does the author say have provided taxpayer dollars for embryonic stem cell research?
3. According to the author New York introduced a stem cell research initiative that would provide how much money annually to its research center?

I n August 2001, President George [W.] Bush limited federal spending on human embryonic stem-cell research to stem-cell lines derived before that date. President Bush said that he was restricting federal support for research to those lines because he did not want to "encourage further destruction of human embryos that have at least the potential for life." So far only 22 stem-cell lines qualify for federal funding of human embryonic stem-cell research, and the National Institutes of Health provided only $24.3 million last year for such research. It's impossible to tell what the level of federal funding for such research would be now in the absence of the administration's restrictions, because it is impossible to know how many good solid research proposals those restrictions have deterred from even being submitted.

State Governments Are Funding Stem Cell Research

However, these federal funding restrictions have provoked an outpouring of state initiatives for research funding for stem-cell research. So far four states have put taxpayer dollars behind human embryonic stem-cell research. The 800 pound gorilla in the stem cell funding arena is California. Last November [2004], California voters passed a $3 billion initiative that created the new California Institute of Regenerative Medicine that aims to fund stem-cell research at $300 million annually for the next ten years. That is more than 12 times higher than current federal funding. California will not only be outspending

Commercial stem cell research, like the work being done by the Geron Corporation, has increased and so has private funding for academic research.

FAST FACT

According to the Center for American Progress, the state of California plans to spend more than $1.8 billion on embryonic stem cell research by the year 2018.

the U.S. Federal government; it will be trouncing whole countries on stem-cell research funding. For example, the United Kingdom has plans to spend $175 million per year on stem-cell research. In 2002, the Australian government awarded the Australia Stem Cell Centre with $43.55 million over four years. And the research of South Korean scientists who have recently been making breakthroughs in cloning human embryonic stem cells has been supported by about $11 million in government grants.

The other three states that have ponied up for stem-cell research are New Jersey, Connecticut, and Illinois. New Jersey has allocated $150 million to construct a new stem-cell research center, and Governor Richard Codey is proposing a November 2006 referendum to ask voters to authorize $230 million to fund the research. Connecticut has passed legislation authorizing $100 million in spending on both adult and embryonic stem-cell research over the next 10 years. In Illinois, Governor Rod Blagojevich moved $10 million of state public health research funding to establish a new stem-cell research institute called the Illinois Regenerative Medicine Institute. This was in lieu of a much more ambitious plan by state Comptroller Dan Hynes, who proposed a $1 billion referendum to create an Illinois Regenerative Medicine Institute that would have dispensed $100 million a year in research grants and loans over the next 10 years. The proposal would have been funded by a 6 percent tax on face-lifts, Botox injections and other cosmetic procedures.

State Governments Are Increasingly Proposing to Fund Stem Cell Research

Many other states are mulling over various proposals to fund stem-cell research. In Massachusetts, legislators are expected to introduce a bill proposing that the state spend $100 million on stem-cell research. In North Carolina, a bill proposing to use $10 million from the state's tobacco settlement proceeds to fund stem-cell research has been introduced in the state legislature. Even in the president's home state, the Texas House of Representatives approved selling $41.1 million in bonds to build a stem-cell research facility at the University of Texas Health Science Center at Houston. (Gov. Rick Perry says that he is against spending taxpayer money on research that ends human life.) In March [2005], legislation was introduced in the New York State Assembly to create the New York State Institute for Stem-Cell Research and Regenerative Medicine with annual funding of $100 million. The Maryland House of Representatives approved a bill allocating $23 million to a stem-cell research Fund—the bill died in

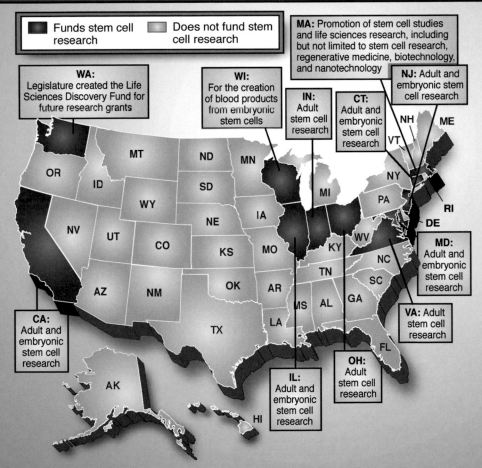

State Funding of Embryonic and Fetal Research, January 2007

Which states have authorized funding for stem cell research?

Funds stem cell research

Does not fund stem cell research

MA: Promotion of stem cell studies and life sciences research, including but not limited to stem cell research, regenerative medicine, biotechnology, and nanotechnology

WA: Legislature created the Life Sciences Discovery Fund for future research grants

WI: For the creation of blood products from embryonic stem cells

IN: Adult stem cell research

CT: Adult and embryonic stem cell research

NJ: Adult and embryonic stem cell research

CA: Adult and embryonic stem cell research

MD: Adult and embryonic stem cell research

VA: Adult stem cell research

IL: Adult and embryonic stem cell research

OH: Adult stem cell research

Taken from: State Embryonic and Fetal Research Laws, National Conference of State Legislatures, January 19, 2007. Available at www.ncsl.org/programs/health/genetics/embfet.htm.

the state Senate. A bill creating the Pennsylvania stem-cell research council that would disburse the research funding created through a $500 million bond initiative paid for by a 2 percent tax on medical devices and diagnostic equipment has been introduced in the Pennsylvania State House.

Private Funding Is Increasing Stem Cell Research at Academic Institutions

Setting aside commercial efforts like those of the Geron Corporation, private funding for academic stem-cell research is also rising. For example, the Starr Foundation is providing $50 million over three years for human embryonic stem-cell research at three New York City medical institutions, including the Sloan-Kettering Memorial Cancer Center. The Harvard University Stem Cell Institute is seeking $100 million in private funding. The University of California, Los Angeles announced the establishment of its Institute for Stem Cell Biology and Medicine with $20 million in funding over the next 5 years. Stanford University announced the creation of $120 million Institute for Cancer/Stem Cell Biology and Medicine in 2002. Former Intel CEO Andy Grove gave the University of California in San Francisco a matching grant of $5 million to start its Developmental and Stem Cell Biology Program. In 2001, an anonymous donor gave Johns Hopkins University in Baltimore a $58.5 million gift to launch an Institute for Cell Engineering. The University of Minnesota has set up a Stem Cell Institute with a $15 million capital grant. In 2004, a grateful patient pledged $25 million over the next ten years to finance stem-cell research at the University of Texas Health Science Center in Houston.

Federal Funding of Stem Cell Research May Not Be Necessary

Given all of these sources of funding for stem-cell research, it's a real question whether or not researchers need the Feds at this point. And one more deliciously ironic thought: It's just possible that, by imposing his funding restrictions and spurring so many independent initiatives, President Bush has actually caused the creation of more embryonic stem cell lines than would have been produced with federal funding.

Viewpoint

4

Stem Cell Research Policies Hurt the United States

Barbara A. Mikulski

"Without national standards, this research will be conducted outside of the public eye and without national scrutiny."

In the following viewpoint Barbara A. Mikulski argues that current stem cell research policies hold the United States back. Restrictions on federal funding have stopped stem cell research from advancing and have prevented the discovery of treatments and cures for some of America's worst diseases, she explains. Millions of American lives could be saved if stem cell researchers were allowed more funding and increased access to stem cell lines. Furthermore, she warns that America risks losing some of its best scientists to other countries because they cannot get funding to perform their research. Meanwhile, other research is occurring in unregulated private firms, and the author is skeptical of its quality and methodology. Mikulski concludes that America needs a strong na-

Barbara A. Mikulski, "Stem Cell Research Is About Saving Lives, Not Party Lines," in U.S. Senate, April 11, 2007.

tional policy that incorporates sound science and ethical principles for the benefit of all Americans.

Barbara A. Mikulski has served as a Democratic senator from Maryland since 1986. Actively involved in various health issues, she supports an expansion in the federal funding of stem cell research under medical and ethical guidelines.

AS YOU READ, CONSIDER THE FOLLOWING QUESTIONS:

1. In what way do American scientists have their hands tied behind their backs, according to the author?
2. To what countries are American scientists going to pursue stem cell research?
3. What does "intellectual capital" mean in the context of this viewpoint?

I rise today to speak with great urgency on the need to pass the Stem Cell Research Enhancement Act of 2007. We must pass this bill. Every year we wait to pass this bill, our research falls three years behind. That's another patient who may have been saved, another family that may not have to watch a loved one suffer. Stem cell research is very important to the American public. It's very important in Maryland, and it's very important to me. I am a firm, clear, unabashed supporter of stem cell research. We must move this bill forward. We need a national framework to establish bioethical standards based on sound science and ethical principles.

Stem Cell Research Can Save Lives

Stem cell research has the potential to save lives—improving the prevention, diagnosis, and treatment of diseases. It has the potential to help find cures for some of life's most devastating diseases: Alzheimer's disease, Parkinson's disease, diabetes, heart disease, multiple sclerosis, spinal cord injury. Just imagine if scientists could find a cure for Alzheimer's or give individuals a longer cognitive stretch out. Think of the savings we could have by investing in stem cell research. Imagine what this research could mean to our returning veterans, coming home with traumatic brain injuries. There are a cornucopia of new opportunities for new breakthroughs.

This is not about ideology. It's not about party. It is about our American people. What we can invent could help save lives everywhere.

Federal Restrictions Hinder Stem Cell Research

Yesterday [April 10, 2007] I met with scientists at Johns Hopkins University [in Baltimore, Maryland] to discuss breakthrough stem cell research. I wanted to be sure that I was on the right track. I said to the scientists: "tell me what you are doing and tell me what impedes you now, working under the Bush framework." Well, they gave me an ear full.

There are great things going on at Hopkins—studies that may one day help prevent the rejection of transplanted organs such as the kidney and pancreas. Dr. Douglass Kerr is doing breakthrough work, restoring movement to paralyzed rats and showing the potential of embryonic stem cells to restore function to humans suffering from stroke. This could possibly even aid those soldiers who are returning from Iraq and Afghanistan.

Private and state funds cannot be a substitute for the necessary federal investment. I am proud that Maryland passed stem cell legislation last year, and the General Assembly just approved $23 million for next year. But it can't be a substitute for federal funds.

Right now, scientists have their hands tied behind their backs. Cell lines that can be used for research now are deficient and defective. They need access to other lines that are currently off limits due to the President's restrictions. Right now, Hopkins scientists can not even collaborate on the stem cell work they are doing. This goes against the way science is studied, slowing down potential breakthroughs.

Our country is sitting back while other countries are moving forward. Scientists are going to other countries to do this research—

The United States has more restrictive stem cell research policies than many of its competitors.

Permissive: allows various embryonic stem cell derivation techniques, including somatic cell nuclear transfer (SCNT), also called research or therapeutic cloning. SCNT is the transfer of a cell nucleus from a somatic or body cell into an egg from which the nucleus has been removed.

Somewhat restrictive: allows research on imported emybronic stem cell lines only or on a limited number of previously established stem cell lines.

Flexible: allows derivations permitted from fertility clinic donations only, excluding SCNT, and often under certain restrictions. Research is permitted only on remaining embryos no longer needed for reproduction.

Very restrictive: research generally banned.

No official policy

Taken from: William Hoffman, MBBNet, University of Minnesota.

China, Singapore, Australia, Germany. We are losing our intellectual capital. We are losing young scientists who are choosing other paths because of restraints. We are losing our best and brightest to other countries instead of supporting them here in the United States.

Federal Restrictions Lead to Unregulated Stem Cell Research

This research has been operating with one hand tied behind its back. Scientists have been prohibited from doing new stem cell research.

Six years ago, the President restricted federal funding for embryonic stem cell research in the most narrow way. The decision created an enormous loophole for researchers in private, for-profit making firms in an unregulated atmosphere. The result—federally funded stem cell research was halted almost entirely. Stem cell research was conducted by private entities with no federal bioethical standards.

This research must be conducted in the sunshine. We need a national framework to establish bioethical standards based on sound science and ethical principles. Without national standards, this research will be conducted outside of the public eye and without national scrutiny. This is where I fear dark and ghoulish things can occur.

A biotechnologist conducts stem cell research in Singapore. The author of this viewpoint argues that the United States is falling behind other countries in research.

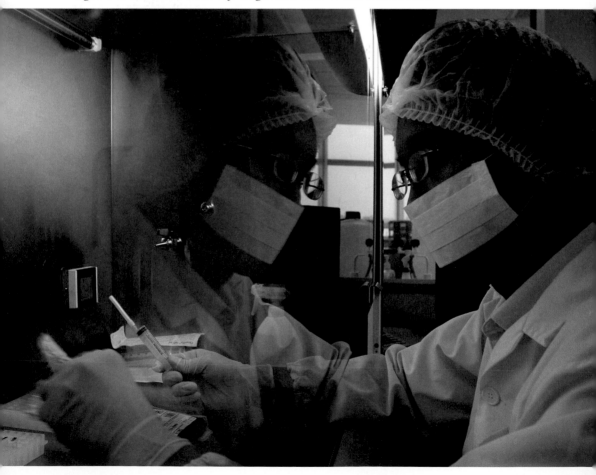

I acknowledge the validity of some of the issues that have been raised. But as long as you shove it underground, as long as you shove it behind closed doors, then you're going to get either faulty research or very bad ethics.

Stem Cell Research Requires a National Framework

Our legislation will remove the restrictions imposed by the President that have effectively stopped this research. It provides the ethical and medical framework for federally funded stem cell research, and allows for sound science and sound ethics. It creates strong ethical guidelines for expanded federal stem cell research and ensures that research is conducted within a rigorous ethical framework, providing transparency and public accountability. The bill expands scientists' access to stem cell lines currently off-limits to federal funding now. It creates a strong national framework that will advance the science of stem cell research and allows for the national collaboration necessary to promote advancement in research that is being done across the country and around the world.

We heard what the voters said in November [2006]. "Change the direction of the country," they said. Change the priorities. I am on the side of cures and research. I am proud to support stem cell research that will save lives. We have heard the American public's outcry and I believe we must heed their call. We cannot continue to wait any longer.

EVALUATING THE AUTHOR'S ARGUMENTS:

In the viewpoint you just read, Barbara A. Mikulski asserts that U.S. stem cell research polices do not serve the American people. Consider the effects of the current policies on the American people. What suggestions would you offer for changing stem cell research policy so that the United States can competitively pursue research?

Stem Cell Research Policies Do Not Hurt the United States

Eric Cohen

"[It is] disingenuous to claim that America is 'falling behind' when it remains, by far, the world's leader in stem-cell science."

In the following viewpoint Eric Cohen argues that federal stem cell research policies do not hurt the United States. In fact, he claims the United States has one of the strongest stem cell research programs in the world. Cohen explains that since 1998 America has produced more than 46 percent of the published research on the matter, while the remaining 54 percent is divided among seventeen countries. Furthermore, 85 percent of stem cell lines developed in America have been used worldwide. Even more important, Cohen argues that America's stem cell policies are designed to respect human dignity while addressing ethical dilemmas surrounding the research. American policy aims to find a balance between health and science so that stem cell research can be advanced without the destruction of embryos. The

Eric Cohen, "Celling Spin: The Reasonableness of the Bush Policy, and the Unreasonableness of Its Critics," *National Review*, May 3, 2006. Reproduced by permission.

author concludes that U.S. policy on stem cell research is often misunderstood, but it was created in the best interests of the American people.

Eric Cohen is editor of the *New Atlantis,* a journal that aims to clarify the nation's moral and political understanding of technology. He also serves as director of the Bioethics and American Democracy program at the Ethics and Public Policy Center, an institute dedicated to applying the Judeo-Christian moral tradition to critical issues of public policy.

AS YOU READ, CONSIDER THE FOLLOWING QUESTIONS:

1. According to the author, in what year was there a "growth spurt" in stem cell research publications by American scientists?

2. What country produces the second-largest amount of stem cell research publications, as reported by Cohen?

3. What does Cohen say is the main point of the Bush administration's stem cell policy?

F or connoisseurs of stem-cell spin, recent weeks have offered a feast. In its April 2006 issue, the journal *Nature Biotechnology* published a short paper entitled "An international gap in human ES [embryonic-stem] cell research." The authors, Jason Owen-Smith of the University of Michigan and Jennifer McCormick of Stanford, carefully reviewed all scientific publications involving the use or derivation of human embryonic stem-cells, starting with the very first paper in 1998 and ending just over a year ago.

FAST FACT

According to *The Scientist* magazine, a 2006 study found that between 2000 and 2004, 42 percent of all stem cell research was published by Americans.

Their aim, very clear in the tone and tenor of the text, was to show that American stem-cell scientists were falling behind their counterparts abroad, and that the [George W.] Bush administration's funding policy was to blame. "Expanding the purview of federal [human embryonic-stem] cell funding can still prevent the United States from slipping off the leading edge of developments in this vital field," the authors write. A press release accompanying the article breathlessly proclaims that "the fear that United States researchers might lose ground to their international counterparts in human embryonic stem cell research now appears to have become a fact."

American Scientists Are Not Falling Behind in Stem Cell Research

Coverage of the study took much the same tone. "The United States is falling behind other countries in human embryonic-stem-cell research," reported UPI. The *Washington Post* began its brief report on the study by telling its readers "American scientists are falling behind researchers elsewhere in stem cell discoveries because of U.S. limits on the use of federal funding, a study has found."

The study itself, however, tells a very different story. Owen-Smith and McCormick reviewed the 132 human embryonic stem cell articles published in 55 scientific journals since 1998. Far from showing the United States lagging behind in the field, they found that American scientists had by far the most publications—46 percent of the total, while the other 54 percent were divided among scientists from 17 other countries. They also found that the number of papers in the field published by Americans has increased each year, with a particularly notable growth spurt beginning in 2002.

How, then, to support the image of Americans "falling behind"? The best the authors could do was to note that, as their accompanying press release claims, "human embryonic stem cell research has been accelerating at a faster pace internationally." They point out that while in 2002 a third of the papers published in the world came from the U.S., in 2004 only a quarter did. Their data also show, however, that in 2002 there were only 10 papers published on human embryonic stem cells (of which 3 were American), while in 2004 there were 77 papers, of which 20 were American. So the number of American publications in the field was nearly seven times greater in 2004 than it was in 2002—a trend that hardly supports the image of research stifled or held back by government policy.

To advance the perception of American science in crisis, Owen-Smith and McCormick compare the output of American scientists to that of their counterparts in the rest of the world combined, hoping to obscure the inconvenient fact that no single country comes close to challenging America's dominance of embryonic stem-cell research.

Another recent study, highlighted by *The Scientist* magazine in March 2006, found the same to be the case in the larger field of stem-cell research. Between 2000 and 2004, 42 percent of all scientific publications in stem-cell research were by Americans. Our nearest competitor was Germany, far behind with only 10 percent of the total.

American Stem Cell Lines Are Used Worldwide

But the most extraordinary aspect of the Owen-Smith and McCormick study—which the authors conveniently and deliberately fail to highlight—was what it said about the use of those embryonic-stem-cell lines approved for federal funding under President Bush's 2001

Geron Corporation's CEO Tom Okarma contends that President Bush's stem cell lines are entirely usable in research.

policy. Besides claiming that America is falling behind, critics of the Bush policy have argued relentlessly that the presidentially approved lines are inadequate or even useless. But this claim is also severely undermined by the study.

Grudgingly, and almost in passing, Owen-Smith and McCormick note that "Only 14.4% (19) of publications described the use or derivation of lines not approved by the NIH [National Institutes of Health]." In other words, more than 85 percent of all the published embryonic-stem-cell research in the world has used the lines approved for funding under the Bush policy. Since this is almost twice the number of papers published by Americans, it is clear that a great deal of the work done abroad has also involved these lines, even though most of it could not have been funded by the NIH. The lines are used, in other words, because they are useful, not only because they are eligible for federal support.

Many critics of the Bush policy claim that the Bush lines are useless because they are contaminated with mouse-feeder cells. This claim also seems largely specious. Two recent studies have shown methods of culturing the NIH-funded lines that leave them free of all trace of animal materials. Discussing his company's use of the Bush-approved lines, Geron CEO Tom Okarma recently, told Wired News, "the stuff you hear published that all of those lines are irrevocably contaminated with mouse materials and could never be used in people—hogwash. If you know how to grow them, they're fine."

Last month [in April 2006] the *Wall Street Journal* reported similar sentiments from other researchers in the field. While scientists would always welcome more funding for their work (who wouldn't?), those reached by the *Journal* seem not to see Bush's policy as the intolerable impediment his political opponents suggest it is. "There is a lot going on in the U.S.," said Renee Reijo-Pera, co-director of the Human Embryonic Stem Cell Center at the University of California, San Francisco. "The official story [of stem-cell advocates] is how we are falling behind in tragedy and dismay. And I don't think that is the case."

U.S. Stem Cell Policy Addresses Ethical Dilemmas

Of course, the argument for the Bush administration's funding policy does not finally rest on scientific utility but on moral and democratic principle. As the president has put it: "We should not use public money to support the further destruction of human life." This means that some types of research, even if beneficial, should never be conducted with federal dollars. The current limit would not move—and the moral principle it upholds would not change—even if it were true that it "crippled" American stem-cell science. And supporters of the Bush policy should be upfront about the fact that some useful research may not advance as quickly or at all, at least in America, because of such limits. Surely more could be done, and more quickly, if more

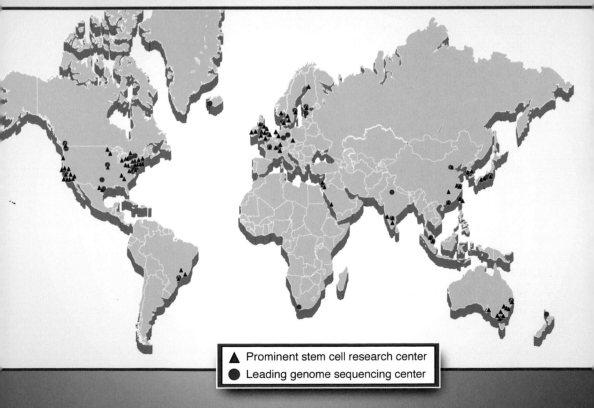

Global Stem Cell Research Centers

Many of the world's prominent stem cell research centers are located in the United States.

▲ Prominent stem cell research center
● Leading genome sequencing center

Taken from: Minnesota Biomedical and Bioscience Network (MBBNet), University of Minnesota Medical School.

public dollars were spent on more lines—that is, if the profound ethical dilemmas involved were simply ignored.

That said, it is dishonest to obscure the useful research that the Bush policy has indeed facilitated, and disingenuous to claim that America is "falling behind" when it remains, by far, the world's leader in stem-cell science. Rather than make the narrow case for funding embryo-destructive research, many opponents of the Bush policy zealously claim that the Bush policy "stops" all useful research. In doing so, they wrongly suggest that scientific advance and ethical boundaries are fundamentally opposed to one another, or they ignore the moral issue entirely, treating stem-cell policy as if it were entirely a scientific question to be settled by scientific data.

American Stem Cell Policy Respects Human Dignity

The point of the Bush policy, for all its many limitations and drawbacks, is to show that science can proceed without violating human dignity or destroying nascent human life, even if it cannot proceed as quickly and by as many simultaneous routes. The choice it offers is not between science and ethics, but between a devotion to science and health so total that it abandons all ethical limits, and a devotion to science and health balanced and constrained by a respect for human equality and dignity, and committed to a culture of life largely understood.

Opponents of the policy usually avoid taking on that basic ethical principle, and so they have offered up various practical arguments against the scientific utility of the policy: the lines are contaminated, there are not enough to support research, they are causing American researchers to fall behind their foreign counterparts. Being practical arguments, these assertions must stand up to factual scrutiny. And so far, the evidence suggests they mostly do not.

One can make reasonable arguments for a more permissive funding policy; one cannot reasonably claim that the policy is wreaking havoc on American science, or that America is becoming backward because only private dollars or state funds are available for the derivation of stem cells from destroyed human embryos. To make such a claim is not science or even the rational defense of science; it is fundamentalism in the name of science, employing the most unscientific means imaginable: playing with the data to advance one's cause.

The United States' Stem Cell Policies Are Advancing Science

All things considered, the Bush policy still looks reasonable as it approaches its five-year anniversary. It is helping useful science advance without making embryo destruction a national project and without trampling on the deepest values of those citizens who believe (with good rational arguments) that embryo destruction is a grave wrong. The fight over the policy has also shown, sadly, that the self-proclaimed defenders of reason cannot always be counted on to be reasonable themselves.

EVALUATING THE AUTHORS' ARGUMENTS:

In this viewpoint Eric Cohen argues that the United States has strong and successful stem cell research policies that have enabled America to lead the world in stem cell research. How do you think the author of the preceding viewpoint, Barbara A. Mikulski, might respond to this argument? Explain your answer using evidence from the texts.

Facts About Stem Cell Research

Editors' note: These facts can be used in reports or papers to reinforce or add credibility when making important points or claims.

Important Discoveries in Stem Cell Research

- 1960s: Scientists present evidence of ongoing stem cell activity in the brain.
- 1963: Self-renewing cells are discovered in the bone marrow of mice.
- 1968: Bone marrow transplant between two siblings successfully treats Severe Combined Immunodeficiency (SCID).
- 1978: Hematopoietic stem cells (which are responsible for creating all components of blood cells) are discovered in human cord blood.
- 1981: Embryonic stem cells are culled from the inner cell mass of mice. The term *embryonic stem cell* is coined by scientist Gail Martin.
- 1992: Neural stem cells are cultured in vitro.
- 1997: Leukemia is found to originate in hematopoietic stem cells—the first direct evidence of cancer stem cells.
- 1998: The first human embryonic stem cell line is derived at the University of Wisconsin–Madison by James Thomson and coworkers.
- 2001: The first early (four- to six-cell stage) human embryos are cloned at Advanced Cell Technology for the purpose of generating embryonic stem cells.
- 2005: Researchers at Kingston University in England discover cord-blood-derived embryonic-like stem cells (CBEs), which are found in umbilical cord blood. These cells are able to differentiate into more types of tissue than adult stem cells.
- August 2006: Kazutoshi Takahashi and Shinya Yamanaka discover that pluripotent stem cells can be induced in rats.

- October 2006: Scientists in England create the first-ever artificial liver cells using umbilical cord blood stem cells.
- June 2007: Normal skin cells are found to be capable of being reprogrammed to an embryonic state in mice.
- October 2007: Mario Capecchi, Martin Evans, and Oliver Smithies win the 2007 Nobel Prize for Physiology or Medicine for their work on mouse embryonic stem cells.
- November 2007: Human-induced pluripotent stem cells are created, making it possible to produce a stem cell from almost any other human cell instead of relying on embryos.
- January 2008: Human embryonic stem cell lines are generated without destruction of the embryo.

Stem Cell Research Policies in the United States

On August 9, 2001, President George W. Bush announced his decision to allow federal funds to be used only on existing human embryonic stem cell lines.

Since then the following criteria must be met in order for embryonic stem cell research to be eligible for federal funding:

- The derivation process had already been initiated on the stem cell lines, meaning the removal of the inner cell mass from the blastocyst had already been started.
- The embryo from which the stem cell line was derived was no longer capable of developing into a human being.
- The stem cells must have been derived from an embryo that was created for reproductive purposes.
- The embryo could no longer be needed for reproductive purposes.
- The donation of the embryo must have been obtained with informed consent.
- No financial inducements were provided for donation of the embryo.

According to the National Institutes of Health (NIH), there were sixty-four cell lines in existence as of August 9, 2001, at the following ten laboratories:

- BresaGen, Inc., Athens, Georgia (4 lines)
- CyThera, Inc., San Diego, California (9 lines)

- Karolinska Institute, Stockholm, Sweden (5 lines)
- Monash University, Melbourne, Australia (6 lines)
- National Center for Biological Sciences, Bangalore, India (3 lines)
- Reliance Life Sciences, Mumbai, India (7 lines)
- Technion-Israel Institute of Technology, Haifa, Israel (4 lines)
- University of California, San Francisco, California (2 lines)
- Göteborg University, Göteborg, Sweden (19 lines)
- Wisconsin Alumni Research Foundation, Madison, Wisconsin (5 lines)

According to Genetics and Public Policy, the following are key events in the development of stem cell policies in the United States:

- 1994: The NIH establishes the Human Embryo Research Panel, which recommends federal funding for embryo research.
- 1996: Congress passes the Dickey-Wicker Amendment banning NIH funding of human embryo research.
- 2000: The NIH releases guidelines allowing federal funding for human embryonic stem cells derived in the private sector.
- 2001: President George W. Bush allows federal funding of stem cell research on embryos that are already in existence and have been left over from fertility clinics. NIH launches the Human Embryonic Stem Cell Registry, which lists all the cell lines eligible for federally funded research.
- 2004: The Stem Cell Research Enhancement Act of 2004 is introduced into the House of Representatives. It would relax limits on federal funding of embryonic stem cell research.
- 2004: Californians pass Proposition 71, which allows the state to spend $3 billion over ten years to fund stem cell research.
- 2004: NIH announced plans to develop a National Stem Cell Bank that would consolidate some of the available embryonic cell lines into one location.
- 2005: The following bills are introduced into Congress to support funding of alternatives to embryonic stem cell research: the Cord Blood Stem Cell Act of 2005, the Joe Testaverde Adult Stem Cell Research Act of 2005, and the Respect for Life Pluripotent Stem Cell Act of 2005.

- 2005: Congress passes the Stem Cell Research Enhancement Act of 2005, which would loosen restrictions on federal funding of embryonic stem cell research.
- 2005: The state of New Jersey announces it will fund a $150 million stem cell research center.
- 2006: President George W. Bush vetoes the Stem Cell Research Enhancement Act of 2005.
- 2007: In January 2007 the House and Senate again pass the Stem Cell Research Enhancement Act. The president vetoes it.
- 2007: President George W. Bush offers his support of legislation that would expand existing federal funding of embryonic stem cell research to embryos that have ceased developing in laboratory conditions.
- 2008: Many embryonic stem cell researchers and their supporters look to the 2008 presidential race, in which stem cells are likely to be a pivotal issue.

Facts About Embryonic Stem Cells

According to the International Society for Stem Cell Research (ISSCR), the following qualities define human embryonic stem cells:

- Embryonic stem cells are like blank slates and are capable of developing into the specialized cells that create bone, nerve, and other tissues in the human body.
- They are located in the inner cell mass of a blastocyst.
- A blastocyst forms about five days after the egg has been fertilized.
- A blastocyst is approximately one-tenth the size of the head of a pin.
- A blastocyst has not yet implanted itself into the uterus.

According to MSNBC research:

- Number of unused in vitro fertilization (IVF) embryos that supporters claim are available for research: 400,000
- Number of all unused IVF embryos not reserved for future implantation or destruction: 11,200
- Number of those embryos estimated to be usable for research: approximately 3,600

- Annual federal budget to publicize "embryo adoption" as an alternative to research or destruction: $1 million
- Number of donated embryos that are known to have been carried through to live birth: 81

Facts About Alternatives to Embryonic Stem Cells
- According to the *Wall Street Journal,* only two of fifteen biotech companies devoted to stem cell research in the United States in 2001 were devoted to embryonic stem cell research. The other thirteen were researching adult stem cells or umbilical cord stem cells.
- Adult bone marrow stem cells can form bone, muscle, fat, liver, and neural tissues.
- The *Journal of the American Medical Association* published a story about thirty-three lupus patients who have not experienced lupus symptoms since receiving a bone marrow transplant containing their own adult stem cells.
- On September 21, 2006, the *Los Angeles Times* reported that German scientists used adult stem cells to improve heart function in patients who had suffered heart attacks in the past.
- On January 7, 2007, *Newsweek* reported that researchers discovered that stem cells found in amniotic fluid can be turned into a variety of cell types, can divide quickly, can survive for long periods of time, and do not turn into tumors.
- In February 2007 the *Guardian* reported that researchers in Spain had used stem cells from the fat of a patient to treat the patient's heart.

Stem Cell Research Policies Around the World
Australia
- Australian policies are more relaxed compared with other nations.
- Recent laws have been approved for therapeutic cloning.
- Reproductive cloning is strictly condemned.
- Embryos cloned for therapeutic use may not be implanted in a womb and must be discarded within two weeks.
Canada
- Canadian laws are somewhat flexible in the field of stem cell research.

- In 2005 roughly $5 million dollars were directed for experiments replacing damaged cells in the heart, lungs, or blood vessels with adult stem cells.
- Leftover embryos from failed in vitro fertilization procedures may be used.
- Therapeutic cloning is not allowed. It is unacceptable to create embryos for the purpose of utilizing stem cells, since the embryo is destroyed after the extraction of stem cells.

European Union (EU)
- The EU does not directly fund stem cell research that results in embryonic destruction.
- The EU funds other stem cell research areas if it is independently approved and deemed ethically acceptable.
- Policies vary within Europe, and the majority of stem cell research is funded by individual nations.
- The primary funding for stem cell research in the EU is directed toward adult stem cells.
- Top stem cell research supporters are the United Kingdom, Sweden, and Belgium.

Germany, Austria, and Italy
- Policies regarding stem cell research are much stricter than in other nations.
- Research involving embryonic stem cells is either prohibited or severely restricted.
- In 2006 Germany pushed for a ban on all embryonic stem cell research in the EU.

South Korea
- South Korea has very flexible policies regarding research. As such, it has made strong advancements in stem cell research.
- South Korea's stem cell research policies are not supported by all nations.
- South Korean researchers have been able to successfully produce stem cells that are a perfect genetic match to patients of all races and both genders.

- South Korea's progress in therapeutic cloning has allowed researchers efficiently to produce stem cells tailored to the individual and with a low risk of immunological rejection.

Spain
- Originally, scientists were allowed to use only embryos frozen prior to 2003.
- In 2003 Spain decided that embryos available for research could also include embryos frozen within two weeks of conception.
- Spain allows parents who have children with incurable diseases to conceive a new embryo and utilize stem cells to treat their children, thereby providing a tissue donor. This procedure is used only after all other options have been exhausted, so it is not a primary means for treatment.

Switzerland
- Switzerland allows unused embryonic stem cells that would otherwise be discarded following in vitro fertilization to be used.
- Swiss laws strongly prohibit reproductive cloning or the creation of an embryo specifically for stem cell research purposes.

United Kingdom (UK)
- The UK government created policies based on the premise that stem cell research provides vast potential to create new treatments for many serious diseases such as diabetes and heart disease.
- In 2004–2005 the government directed approximately £25 million into research and other areas such as the UK Stem Cell Bank.
- In 2005 the UK Stem Cell Initiative (UKSCI) set out to construct a ten-year plan for stem cell research, encouraging both public and private funding.
- Due to the UKSCI's recommendations, the public sector funding for stem cell research over 2006–2007 and 2007–2008 will have increased to £100 million.

United States
- The United States generally limits federal funding for embryonic stem cell research.
- It supports a small number of pre-2001 stem cell lines produced from embryos left over following in vitro fertilization.

- Private funding is allowed, and the United States does not limit and regulate state and local funds.

The Future of Embryonic Stem Cells

- Embryonic stem cells have been used to treat spinal cord injuries, according to Johns Hopkins University.
- Embryonic stem cells have slowed vision loss in studies with mice, according to the *Washington Post*.
- The *Washington Post* reported that embryonic stem cells have been shown to reverse some symptoms of Parkinson's disease.
- Cardiovascular precursor cells have been created from embryonic stem cells and could lead to treatments for heart disease, according to a *New Scientist* article.
- *Science Daily* reported that embryonic stem cell studies predict T-cells could lead to a cure for AIDS.
- The Center for American Progress fellow Jonathan Moreno says that embryonic stem cells have been used to create insulin-secreting cells that might lead to a cure for diabetes.

Glossary

adult stem cells: Undifferentiated cells that have the potential to become a limited number of specific cell types. These multipotent cells are found in small quantities in umbilical cord blood and adult tissues.

amniotic stem cells: Cells found in the amniotic fluid that surrounds a fetus. Although they are not pluripotent like embryonic stem cells, they can differentiate into more cell types than adult stem cells can.

blastocyst: A thin-walled, hollow structure in early embryonic development that contains a cluster of about 150 cells. It is produced by cell division following fertilization and before implantation in the uterus. It is composed of an outer layer of cells that will become the placenta—a fluid-filled cavity—and an inner cell mass.

cell-based therapies: Treatments used to induce stem cells to differentiate into a specific cell type in order to repair damaged or destroyed cells or tissues.

cell culture: Cells grown in an artificial medium for experimental research.

clone: To generate identical copies of a molecule, cell, or organism.

cloning: The process of genetic duplication.

cord blood stem cells: Stem cells collected from the umbilical cord after birth that can produce all of the blood cells in the body. Cord blood is currently used to treat patients who have undergone chemotherapy as a result of cancers or blood-related disorders.

differentiation: The process by which an undifferentiated embryonic cell acquires the features of a specialized cell such as those found in heart, liver, or muscle tissue.

DNA: Deoxyribonucleic acid, a chemical found primarily in the nucleus of cells. DNA carries the instructions, or blueprint, for making all the structures and materials the body needs to function.

embryo: A group of cells that form after a sperm fertilizes an egg. The embryonic stage ends after eight weeks of gestation in the womb.

embryonic stem cell line: Embryonic stem cells that have been grown in vitro to allow cells to multiply rapidly without differentiation for months to years.

embryonic stem cells: Primitive (undifferentiated) cells derived from a five-day-old embryo prior to implantation in the uterus. They have the potential to become a wide variety of specialized cell types. Embryonic stem cells are not embryos and cannot become a complete organism.

fertilization: The joining of the male sperm and the female egg.

fetus: A developing human from approximately eight weeks after conception until the time of its birth.

gamete: An egg (in the female) or sperm (in the male) cell.

gene: A segment of a chromosome that contains the hereditary information or particular characteristics of a living organism.

in vitro: From the Latin for "in glass"; an artificial environment usually created in a laboratory dish or test tube.

in vitro fertilization: A technique that unites the egg and sperm in a laboratory instead of inside the female body.

inner cell mass (ICM): The cluster of cells inside the blastocyst. These cells give rise to the embryo and ultimately the fetus. The ICM cells are used to generate embryonic stem cells.

multipotent: The capacity for adult cells to become a limited number of types of tissues and cells in the adult body.

plasticity: The ability of stem cells from one adult tissue to generate the differentiated cell types of another tissue.

pluripotent: The ability of a single stem cell to form into any one of the various cell types found in the human body.

reproductive cloning: A technology used to create an animal that has the same DNA as another currently existing animal. A famous example of reproductive cloning is Dolly the sheep—she was created using reproductive cloning techniques.

somatic cell: Any type of body cell other than gametes (egg or sperm).

somatic cell nuclear transfer (SCNT): The replacement of genetic material (nuclear DNA) in an unfertilized egg with genetic material from an adult somatic cell (e.g., skin cell).

somatic stem cells: Non-embryonic stem cells that are not derived from gametes (egg or sperm cells).

stem cells: Cells that have the ability to divide for indefinite periods in culture and to give rise to specialized cells.

therapeutic cloning: The use of cloning technology to help in the search for possible cures and treatments for diseases and disabilities.

undifferentiated: A cell that has not yet generated structures or manufactured proteins characteristic of a specialized cell type.

Organizations to Contact

The editors have compiled the following list of organizations concerned with the issues debated in this book. The descriptions are derived from materials provided by the organizations. All have publications or information available for interested readers. The list was compiled on the date of publication of the present volume; the information provided here may change. Be aware that many organizations take several weeks or longer to respond to inquiries, so allow as much time as possible.

American Association for the Advancement of Science (AAAS)
1200 New York Ave. NW
Washington, DC 20005
(202) 326-6400
e-mail: webmaster@aaas.org • Web site: www.aaas.org

AAAS, an international nonprofit organization, serves as an educator, leader, spokesperson, and professional association dedicated to advancing science around the world. It publishes the journal *Science*, as well as many scientific newsletters, books, and reports. A search of "stem cell research" on its Web site yields numerous articles and publications. AAAS also has an education program that provides students with volunteer opportunities to learn more about what is happening in the world of science and to meet scientists and researchers working in the field.

American Life League (ALL)
PO Box 1350
Stafford, VA 22555
(540) 659-4171 • fax: (540) 659-2586
e-mail: info@all.org • Web site: www.all.org

ALL is an educational pro-life organization that opposes abortion, artificial contraception, reproductive technologies, and fetal experimentation. It asserts that it is immoral to perform experiments on living human embryos and fetuses, whether inside or outside of the mother's womb. Its publications include the brochures *Stem Cell Research: The Science of Human Sacrifice* and *Human Cloning: The Science of Deception.*

American Medical Association (AMA)
515 N. State St.
Chicago, IL 60610
(800) 621-8335
Web site: www.ama-assn.org

The AMA is the largest professional association for medical doctors. It helps set standards for medical education and practices, and it is a powerful lobby in Washington for physicians' interests. The association publishes an e-newsletter as well as journals for many medical fields, including the *Journal of the American Medical Association* (*JAMA*). In addition, searching for "stem cells" on its Web site retrieves numerous articles about stem cell research.

The Center for Bioethics and Human Dignity (CBHD)
2065 Half Day Rd.
Deerfield, IL 60015
(847) 317-8180 • fax: (847) 317-8101
e-mail: info@cbhd.org • Web site: www.cbhd.org

Formed in 1994 by Christian bioethicists, CBHD is an international nonprofit organization that strives to provide research, publications, and teaching to engage leaders in bioethics. The center has initiated a number of projects, including Do No Harm: The Coalition of Americans for Research Ethics, a partnership of researchers, bioethicists, academics, and others that serves as an information clearinghouse on the ethics and science of stem cell research. CBHD maintains the Do No Harm Web site, which advocates for adult stem cell research and other medical technologies that do not involve the destruction of human embryos.

Christian Coalition of America
PO Box 37030
Washington, DC 20013-7030

(202) 479-6900 • fax: (202) 479-4260

Web site: www.cc.org

The Christian Coalition of America is a conservative grassroots political organization that offers Christians a vehicle to become actively involved in shaping their local and national governments. It represents a pro-family agenda and works to educate America about critical issues, including opposing the destruction of human embryos through stem cell research. The Web site provides action alerts, a weekly newsletter, commentary, and voter education information that encourages citizens to vote.

Coalition for the Advancement of Medical Research (CAMR)

2021 K St. NW, Suite 305

Washington, DC 20006

(202) 725-0339

e-mail: CAMResearch@yahoo.com

Web site: www.camradvocacy.org

CAMR is a bipartisan coalition, comprised of more than one hundred nationally recognized patient organizations, universities, scientific societies, and foundations. CAMR focuses on developing better treatments and cures for individuals with life-threatening illnesses and disorders. It periodically performs polls to gauge American response to stem cell research, and its Web site provides links to publications reporting on the most recent developments and events related to stem cell research.

Concerned Women for America (CWA)

1015 Fifteenth St. NW, Suite 1100

Washington, DC 20005

(202) 488-7000 • fax: (202) 488-0806

Web site: www.cwfa.org/main.asp

The CWA is a women's public policy organization that aims to bring the principles of the Bible into all levels of public policy and to restore the nation's moral values. CWA focuses on preserving traditional family values as well as protecting the sanctity of human life. Their Web site has article links, press releases, and legislative alerts.

Council for Responsible Genetics (CRG)
5 Upland Rd., Suite 3
Cambridge, MA 02140
(617) 868-0870 • fax: (617) 491-5344
e-mail: crg@gene-watch.org • Web site: www.gene-watch.org

CRG is a national nonprofit, nongovernmental organization of scientists, health professionals, trade unionists, women's health activists, and others who work to ensure that genetic technologies are developed safely and in the best interest of the public. The council publishes the bimonthly newsletter *Gene Watch* and has several programs that address specific genetics-related issues, including a program called Human Genetic Manipulation and Cloning.

Family Research Council
801 G St. NW
Washington, DC 20001
(202) 393-2100 • fax: (202) 393-2134
Web site: www.frc.org

Family Research Council is a Christian right nonprofit think tank and lobbying organization that promotes the traditional family unit based on Judeo-Christian values. It advocates for national policies that protect traditional notions of marriage and family and the sanctity of human life via books, pamphlets, public events, debates, and testimony. One of its central focuses is on human life and bioethics, and it opposes research that harms, manipulates, or destroys an embryonic human being. It also vigorously supports adult stem cell therapies that can treat patients.

Focus on the Family
8605 Explorer Dr.
Colorado Springs, CO 80920
(800) 232-6459
Web site: www.focusonthefamily.com

Focus on the Family's primary aim is to spread the Gospel of Jesus Christ through a practical outreach to individual families. It is active in promoting social conservative public policy and opposes any activity it deems a threat to the traditional idea of family, including embryonic stem cell research. The organization provides free family counseling, a variety of publications it deems important to family values, and a radio broadcast that reaches 220 million listeners daily in 160 countries.

Genetics Policy Institute (GPI)
11924 Forest Hill Blvd., Suite 22
Wellington, FL 33414
(888) 238-1423 • fax: (561) 791-3889
Web site: www.genpol.org

The Genetics Policy Institute is a nonprofit organization dedicated to establishing a positive legal framework to advance stem cell research. GPI maintains science and legal advisory boards comprised of leading stem cell researchers, disease experts, ethicists, and legal experts and a dedicated full-time staff of policy experts who are available to educate the public and media on stem cell issues.

Harvard Stem Cell Institute (HSCI)
42 Church St.
Cambridge, MA 02138
(617) 496-4050
e-mail: hsci@harvard.edu • Web site: www.hsci.harvard.edu

The HSCI, comprised of Harvard Medical School and eighteen hospitals and research institutions, hosts one of the largest concentrations of biomedical researchers in the world. Its newsletter *Stem Cell Lines* is published three times per year, its monthly newsletter publishes the scientific work of its faculty, and it offers scientific overviews that focus on the use of stem cells and potential therapeutic applications. Topics covered include stem cells and diseases, stem cells and neurodegenerative disease, and type 1 diabetes, to name a few.

The Hastings Center
21 Malcolm Gordon Rd.
Garrison, NY 10524-4125
(845) 424-4040 • fax: (845) 424-4545
e-mail: mail@thehastingscenter.org
Web site: www.thehastingscenter.org

The Hastings Center is an independent, nonpartisan, and nonprofit bioethics research institute. Since its founding in 1969, the center has played a central role in responding to advances in medicine, the biological sciences, and the social sciences by raising ethical questions related to such advances, including stem cell research. The center publishes books, papers, guidelines, and the bimonthly Hastings Center Report.

Institute for Stem Cell Research (ISCR)
School of Biological Sciences
The University of Edinburgh
The Roger Land Building
The King's Buildings
West Mains Rd.
Edinburgh, Scotland, EH9 3JQ
+44 (0) 131 650 5828 • fax: +44 (0) 131 650 7773
e-mail: P.Hope@ed.ac.uk • Web site: www.iscr.ed.ac.uk/index.html

The Institute for Stem Cell Research is a global stem cell research and technology center devoted to developing stem cell therapies that can be used to treat human injury and disease. The center hosts state-of-the-art research and laboratory facilities to accommodate research in stem cell culture and experimental embryology. It also offers regular seminar series, and its Web site provides links to many institutes performing stem cell research internationally.

International Society for Stem Cell Research (ISSCR)
111 Deer Lake Rd., Suite 100
Deerfield, IL 60015
(847) 509-1944 • fax: (847) 480-9282
e-mail: isscr@isscr.org • Web site: www.isscr.org

Formed in 2002, the ISSCR is an independent nonprofit organization created to foster the exchange of information on stem cell research. It publishes a monthly newsletter called the *Pulse*, which provides the latest stem cell research news, schedules of scientific and industry meetings, and other general information useful to scientists working with stem cells. ISSCR is also affiliated with the award-winning journal *Cell Stem Cell*, a forum that covers a wide range of information about stem cell biology research.

New York Stem Cell Foundation
163 Amsterdam Ave., Box 309
New York, NY 10023
(212) 787-4111 • fax: (212) 787-5844
e-mail: info@nyscf.org • Web site: www.nyscf.org

A nonprofit organization dedicated to furthering human embryonic stem cell research by supporting scientists engaged in research, educating the public about the potential of embryonic stem cell research, and establishing state-of-the-art facilities to focus on curing disease. The foundation directs its attention toward a few major diseases that show the most promise for cures, including diabetes, heart disease, cancer, and spinal cord damage. It provides links to recent stem cell news as well as the newsletter and press releases.

Research!America
1101 King St., Suite 520
Alexandria, VA 22314-2960
(800) 366-2873 • fax: (703) 739-2372
e-mail: info@researchamerica.org
Web site: www.researchamerica.org

Research!America is the nation's largest nonprofit public education and advocacy alliance, representing more than five hundred medical, health, and scientific organizations. The goal is to improve awareness about the importance of scientific and medical research for the health of American citizens. The alliance regularly conducts public opinion polls and publishes those results in its annual report, called *America Speaks*. The alliance also provides a monthly newsletter, the *Research Advocate*, which features articles about research funding, research in the news, and advocacy initiatives.

Stem Cell Information
Office of Communications and Public Liaison
National Institutes of Health
1 Center Dr., MSC 0188

Bethesda, MD 20892-0199
(301) 496-5787
e-mail: stemcell@mail.nih.gov
Web site: http://stemcells.nih.gov

Stem Cell Information is the resource for stem cell research for the National Institutes of Health, the federal government's leading biomedical research organization. It provides the latest information on important stem cell research topics as well as current federal policy information. Its Web site provides basic stem cell information, stem cell reports that review the state of research, a glossary, photos and illustrations, and links to related sources.

For Further Reading

Books

Michael Bellomo, *The Stem Cell Divide: The Facts, the Fiction, and the Fear Driving the Greatest Scientific, Political, and Religious Debate of Our Time.* New York: AMACON, 2006. Examines the facts and the myths surrounding stem cell research through interviews of scientists about their accomplishments, current work, and what the future holds for this controversial science.

Cynthia Fox, *Cell of Cells: The Global Race to Capture and Control the Stem Cell.* New York: Norton, 2007. Argues in support of both embryonic and adult stem cell research.

Robert P. George and Christopher Tollefsen, *Embryo: A Defense of Human Life.* New York: Doubleday, 2008. Argues that society should neither condone nor publicly fund embryonic stem cell research on the scientific and philosophical grounds that the state has an ethical obligation to protect all human beings in all stages of biological development.

Stephen S. Hall, *Merchants of Immortality: Chasing the Dream of Human Life Extension.* Boston: Mariner, 2005. Examines how technological pursuits such as stem cell research are thriving in the private business sector.

Eve Herold, *Stem Cell Wars: Inside Stories from the Frontlines.* New York: Palgrave Macmillan, 2007. Argues that it is the moral responsibility of the government to support stem cell research in order to provide treatments and cures for conditions afflicting millions of people.

David Albert Jones, *The Soul of the Embryo: An Enquiry into the Status of the Human Embryo in the Christian Tradition.* London: Continuum, 2005. A defense of the Christian view that life begins at conception and thus should be protected from stem cell research.

Chris Mooney, *The Republican War on Science.* New York: Basic Books, 2006. Argues that the Republican Party has placed politics over science in technological advances like stem cell research, favoring ideologically driven pseudoscience over legitimate research.

Yvonne Perry, *Right to Recover: Winning the Political and Religious Wars over Stem Cell Research in America.* Mequon, WI: Nightengale, 2007. A well-researched book that reveals the many ways in which Americans view embryonic stem cell research.

Ted Peters, *Sacred Cells? Why Christians Should Support Stem Cell Research.* Lanham, MD: Rowman & Littlefield, 2008. Tells the story of three Christian theologians who are in favor of stem cell research.

Christopher Thomas Scott, *Stem Cell Now: A Brief Introduction to the Coming Medical Revolution.* New York: Plume, 2006. An accessible and neutral look at the basics of stem cell research and the political, medical, and religious controversies that surround it.

Bernard van Zyl, *Stem Cells Saved My Life: How to Be Next.* Bloomington, IN: AuthorHouse, 2006. The author's personal account of how stem cell therapies repaired his badly damaged heart.

Periodicals and Internet Sources

Monique Baldwin, "Women Carry Cloning Burden," *Daily Telegraph*, June 19, 2007. www.news.com.au/dailytelegraph/story/0,22049,21926043-5001031,00.html.

Mary Carmichael, "Escaping a Moral Mess: Scientists May Have Found a Way Out of the Quandary Over Whether to Destroy Embryos or Cure People," *Newsweek International*, January 22, 2007.

Jim Doyle, "Standing Up for Stem Cell Research," WTN News, November 16, 2005. http://wistechnology.com/articles/2482/.

David Ewing Duncan, "Vision of the Future," *Fortune International* (Asia Edition), October 29, 2007.

Alex Epstein, "The Religious Right's Culture of Living Death," *Capitalism Magazine*, April 29, 2007. www.capmag.com/article.asp?ID= 4945.

Michael Fragoso, "An Easy Cell," *American Online*, January 29, 2007. http://american.com/archive/2007/january-0107/an-easy-cell/.

Markus Grompe, "Alternative Energy for Embryonic Stem Cell Research," *Nature Online*, October 11, 2007. www.nature.com/stemcells/2007/0710/071011/full/stemcells.2007.100.html.

David P. Gushee, "The Stem-Cell Veto," The Center for Bioethics and Human Dignity, July 20, 2006. www.cbhd.org/resources/stemcells/gushee_2006-07-20.htm.

Michael Humprey, "Advances Don't Quell Stem-Cell Debate," *National Catholic Reporter*, January 11, 2008.

Investor's Business Daily, "Where's the Stem Celebration?" February 19, 2008. www.ibdeditorials.com/IBDArticles.aspx?id=2883156122351676.

Leon R. Kass, "Defending Life and Dignity: How, Finally, to Ban Human Cloning," *Weekly Standard*, February 25, 2008.

Diane Krause, interviewed by Molly Dillon, "Bringing Science with Public Policy," *Yale Scientific Magazine*, Fall 2004. http://research.yale.edu/ysm/article.jsp?articleID=300.

Charles Krauthammer, "The Slope Really Is Slippery, Why We Struggle to Gain Our Moral Footing in Bioethics," *Christianity Today*, March 2007.

———, "Stem Cell Vindication," *Washington Post*, November 30, 2007. www.washingtonpost.com/wp-dyn/content/article/2007/11/29/AR2007112901878.html.

Yuval Levin, "A Middle Ground for Stem Cells," *New York Times*, January 19, 2007. www.nytimes.com/2007/01/19/opinion/19levin.html?_r=1&oref=slogin.

McClatchy-Tribune Business News, "No Welfare for Stem Cell Researchers," February 1, 2008.

Daniel McConchie, "'Ethical' Embryonic Stem Cell Research," The Center for Bioethics and Human Dignity, June 10, 2005. www.cbhd.org/resources/stemcells/mcconchie_2005-06-10.htm.

David A. Prentice, Testimony Before the Mississippi Senate Public Health and Welfare Committee, February 22, 2006. http://stemcellresearch.org/testimony/Prentice-MS-SenateHearing-2006.pdf.

Cathy Ruse, "Missouri Manipulation: Don't Get Conned on Cloning," *National Review Online*, October 12, 2007. http://article.nationalreview.com/?q=ZjliNTUwNjgzNmE1OWU3MTg1OGE3ZjE5ZjM5YzEwNjc.

Michael J. Sandel, "Embryo Ethics," *Boston Globe*, April 8, 2007. www.boston.com/news/globe/ideas/articles/2007/04/08/embryo_ethics/?page=1.

Julian Savulescu, "The Case for Creating Human-Nonhuman Cell Lines," Bioethics Forum, Hastings Center, January 24, 2007. www.bioethicsforum.org/research-cloning-hybrid-embryos.asp.

Peter Slevin, "In Heartland, Stem Cell Research Meets Fierce Opposition," *Washington Post*, August 10, 2005, www.washington post.com/wp-dyn/content/article/2005/08/09/AR2005080900793.html.

Susan L. Solomon and Zach W. Hall, "The Stem Cell Wars Are Not Over," Huffingtonpost.com, November 30, 2007. www.huffingtonpost.com/susan-l-solomon/the-stem-cell-wars-are-no_b_74802.html.

Charlie Spiering, "Doubling Down on Stem Cells: Is Your State in Debt? Try Gambling on Embryonic Research," *National Review Online*, October 30, 2007. http://article.nationalreview.com/?q=MWFmNTV1YTIxMDZhMzA2NTUyOTc5NTU2NjkyMjVhOGQ=&w=MA.

Web Sites

EuroStemCell (www.eurostemcell.org). A virtual European stem cell research portal that provides a broad spectrum of stem cell information, including specialized content for researchers and accessible resources for nonscientists. It provides a forum for critical discussion of the latest stem cell research developments and features a number of short films about stem cell research, ethics, cell culture, and cloning.

Stem Cell Action Network (www.stemcellaction.org). A grassroots volunteer advocacy group comprised of patients and their family and friends that supports the funding of stem cell research. It works with America's scientific and medical organizations in the hope of finding cures for many medical conditions, including Parkinson's, Alzheimer's, juvenile diabetes, and even spinal cord injury. They petition, educate, and vote to advance support for embryonic stem cell research.

Stem Cell Research News (www.stemcellresearchnews.com). An independent commercial Web site that offers several electronic publications about stem cell research. One, *Stem Cell Research News*, is a biweekly that features in-depth nonpartisan reporting about stem cell research, including articles about basic research, therapeutic developments, clinical trials, and U.S. and global stem cell policies. Another, *Stem Cell Lab World*, provides monthly information about new research technologies, products, and services geared toward the stem cell research community.

University of Wisconsin Stem Cell and Regenerative Medicine Center (www.stemcells.wisc.edu/about.html). The University of Wisconsin's center for stem cell and regenerative medicine research. A leader in the field of stem cell research, the school was home to the world's first successful culturing of human embryonic stem cells. The mission of the school is to advance stem cell science through faculty, research efforts, and education.

Index

Ethical limits, on science, 14,
16
Ethics Advisory Board (EAB),
42

F
Family Research Council, 13,
68
Faustman, Denise, 71
Federation of American
Societies for Experimental
Biology, 29–30
Fertility treatments
loss of embryos during, 36
opposition to, 38
Fertilization, as beginning of
life, 26–28
Foege, Dave, 67
Food and Drug Administration
(FDA), 71
Franz, Carol, 67
Frist, Bill, *43*
Funding
of adult stem cell research,
71–72
amount of, *103*
ban on federal, *42, 43*
federal, is needed, 94–100
federal, should not be
allowed, 101–106
increased property taxes and,
104–105
limits on federal, 108
private, 97–98, 103–104,
112
restrictions on, should be
eased, 95–97
state, 97–98, 107–112, *111*

G
Gage, Fred, 91
Gastrointestinal, *69*
Gearhart, John, 29
George, Robert P., 8–9
Geron Corporation, 112
Government
oversight, 98–99
research policies of, do not
hurt U.S., 120–127
restrictions on research by,
hurt U.S., 114–118
should fund stem cell
research, 94–100
should not fund stem cell
research, 101–106
See also Funding
Great Britain, 99, 110
Grove, Andy, 112

H
Hair follicle, *69*
Harvard Stem Cell Institute,
96, 98, 112
Hatch, Orrin, 96
Hawaii, 98
Healy, Bernadine, 81
Hochedlinger, Konrad, 78
Holcberg, David, 47
Human beings
embryos are not, 32–38, 48
embryos as, 8–9, 14, 16,
25–31, 36–37, 40–41
Human Embryo Research
Panel, *42*
Human life
beginning of, 34
meaning of, 7–9

Moral constraints, on medical research, 34
Moral status, of embryos, *35*, *36*
Murder
    embryonic stem cell research as, 39–46
    embryonic stem cell research is not, 47–51

N
National Cord Blood Bank, 71, *72*
National Institutes of Health (NIH), *42*, 61, 71, 98–99
Nazi experiments, 34
New Jersey, 97, 102, 104, 110
New York, 97, 111
Non-embryonic stem cells, effectiveness of in treating disease, 44–45
North Carolina, 98, 110
Nuclear transfer, 76, 79–80, 83–85, *84*
Nuremberg Code, 14
Nurse, Paul, 92

O
Obama, Barack, 53, *56*
Okarma, Tom, 124
O'Rahilly, Ronan, 28–29
Organ transplants, 100
Owen-Smith, Jason, 121–124

P
Parkinson's disorder, 23
Parthenogenesis, 79
Pederson, Roger, 100

Penn, Keone, 68
Pennsylvania, 112
Pelosi, Nancy, 40
Peripheral blood, *69*
Perry, Rick, 111
Personhood
    definition of, 9
    of embryos, 14, 16, 35
Placenta, *69*
Pluripotent cells, 74, 75–78
    See also Induced pluripotent stem cells (iPS)
Polio, 59
Potentiality, 31
Pre-embryo concept, 28–29
President's Council on Bioethics, *42*, *43*
Private funding, 97–98, 103–104, 112
Procreation, 26–27
Property taxes, 104–105
Proposition 71, *43*

Q
Qualified research institutions, 103–104

R
Rabon, Jacki, 67
Ramsey, Paul, 28
RAND Institute, 64
Reijo-Pera, Renee, 124
Religious views
    on conception, 34
    on embryos, 48–49
    on stem cell research, *30*
Reproductive cloning, 13, 68

Picture Credits

AP Images, 44, 93, 105, 109, 123
Luis Enrique Ascui/Reuters/Landov, 118
Graham Barclay/Bloomberg News/Landov, 96
© Deco Images II/Alamy, 49
Scott J. Ferrell/Congressional Quarterly/Getty Images, 22
Image copyright Patrick Hall, 2008. Used under license from
    Shutterstock.com, 8
Sanday Huffaker/Getty Images, 11
Kyodo/Landov, 89
© mediacolor's/Alamy, 75
Image copyright Monkey Business Images, 2008. Used under
    license from Shutterstock.com, 62
© PHOTOTAKE Inc./Alamy, 14, 27
Reuters/Landov, 84
Mark Schiefelbein/Bloomberg News/Landov, 56
Javier Soriano/AFP/Getty Images, 52
Nancy Wegard/Liaison/Getty Images, 35
Roger L. Wollenberg/UPI/Landov, 70